through *the* *fire*

through the fire

Gerald Crabb

WestBow
PRESS
A DIVISION OF THOMAS NELSON

WestBow Press books may be ordered through booksellers or by contacting:

WestBow Press
A Division of Thomas Nelson
1663 Liberty Drive
Bloomington, IN 47403
www.westbowpress.com
1-(866) 928-1240

ISBN: 978-1-4497-2802-1 (hc)
ISBN: 978-1-4497-2801-4 (sc)
ISBN: 978-1-4497-2800-7 (e)

Library of Congress Control Number: 2011917919

Printed in the United States of America

WestBow Press rev. date: 10/17/2011

Contents

Foreword

When I first heard the song "Through the Fire" performed at The Bluebird Café in Nashville, Tennessee, I knew it would touch the souls of many, many people. Gerald Crabb is one of the finest songwriters of our time, and this song is a jewel. In his first book, Crabb gives us a close-up, personal experience with the impact this song has had on the lives of people. You will laugh. You will cry. You will be amazed at what God can do through a song. It will bless you greatly.

Ed Leonard
President
Daywind Records

Introduction

Through The Fire

Isaiah 43:2
When you pass through the waters, I will be with you; and when you pass through the rivers, they will not sweep over you. When you walk through the fire, you will not be burned; the flames will not set you ablaze. (NIV)

I have often wondered as a writer what makes one Christian song that you write any better than the others. All of them are centered on God, the Bible and Christianity. Yet there are definitely some that seem to hit the mark better than others.

Many of the songs that you write are very special to you, the writer. As the master songwriter Dottie Rambo once said: "Your songs are your babies; they are a part of your heart and soul."

I have written roughly four hundred songs. Most of them were carefully written and crafted; yet not all were as well received as others. Some just didn't have the impact—that lasting effect that made you want to hear it again, run out and buy it or download it online.

I have observed how amazing it is that you write and write, searching for that one song that people are going to connect with. Sometimes you write for months, and it never happens. You write about mercy, grace, the cross, and every other fundamental teaching in the Bible. Then you start writing about religious clichés you have so often heard from the TV preachers, billboards and bumper stickers.

Every once in a while it works; it just all seems to come together and a pretty good song is born.

But the greatest of all is when a song is inspired, when the Holy Spirit just seems to drop it into your spirit. It is all so amazing because you know that you didn't come up with just another songwriting idea; it was God-given.

I have enjoyed a few of those experiences.

One afternoon while at my home in Beaver Dam, Kentucky, I sat down at the piano as I began to sense a special inspiration. I began to play and sing, "He never promised the Cross would not be heavy and the hill would not be hard to climb. He never offered our victories without fighting, but he said help would always come in time." That's all that came to me. I waited, but nothing else came. I knew it was a special moment; I felt those chill bumps on my arms.

Thank God—I had remembered to push the "record" button on a little cassette recorder that I always kept near-by. After recording it, I quickly got in the car and drove around searching for someone to share my new song with. I was so excited; I knew this was a special song from God. During the following weeks I tried to finish it, but nothing worked. I wrote verses that I felt were strong, but they just weren't right. One verse I wrote ended up being the first verse of another song called "The Journey."

In the past I had written songs in a few hours, and others in a few minutes, so I couldn't understand what was wrong. I just couldn't seem to pull it together.

Several months later we were doing a concert in Mississippi when a lady holding a young child approached me at the product table and asked if I would pray for her. She proceeded to tell of her situation. The child she was holding, who was about a year old, was scheduled to undergo brain surgery within a few weeks. She was several months pregnant with another child, and just a few weeks earlier, her husband, the children's father, had walked off and left them. My heart sank within me as I brushed away the tears. The last thing she said before we prayed was, "I'm still trusting in the Lord."

I stood in awe at such faith. As she turned and walked into the crowd, it was like the Lord spoke to me and said, "Go home and finish the song; you know what to write about now." I don't know what ever happened to that family. I never saw or heard from that lady again, but God used her situation to help me write a song, a message of hope to people who were going through the toughest times of their lives.

I was so moved by the fact that when sometimes-bad things happen to good people, we don't always understand, we don't always have the answer, but we know that God is always faithful. When I got home, I once again sat at the piano, and this is what I wrote:

So many times I've questioned certain circumstances,
Things I could not understand.
Many times in trials, weakness blurs my vision,
My frustrations get so out of hand.
It's then I am reminded I've never been forsaken,
I've never had to stand one test alone.
As I look at all the victories, the spirit rises up in me,
And it's through the fire my weakness is made strong.

He never promised that the cross would not be heavy,
And the hill would not be hard to climb.
He never offered our victories without fighting,
But he said help would always come in time.
Just remember when you're standing in the valley of decision,
And the adversary says give in.
Just hold on, our Lord will show up,
And he will take you through the fire again.

I know within myself that I would surely perish,
But if I trust the hand of God, He'll shield the flames again.

He never promised that the cross would not be heavy,
And the hill would not be hard to climb.
He never offered our victories without fighting,

But he said help would always come in time.
Just remember when you're standing in the valley of decision,
And the adversary says give in.
Just hold on, our Lord will show up,
And he will take you through the fire again.

During this period I was working on material for a new album. A lot of doors and musical opportunities were beginning to open for my family, The Crabb Family. At that time, we had been on the road conducting revivals and concerts full time for about four years. We were running two buses, traveling with a full band, and were very excited about the new album that was to be titled *Pray*.

Christian Taylor Music, the publishing company that I was affiliated with, had scheduled a songwriters' night for their writers to showcase Christian songs at The Blue Bird Café in Nashville, Tennessee. As I recall, the place was packed with many people from the gospel music industry: booking agents, producers, record label presidents, artists, and DJ's. It was a great turn out for gospel music.

Each writer was to perform a song he or she had written or co-written. Those showcases always made me very nervous, and I would usually end up forgetting about half the lyrics and embarrassing myself. I did a song called "I've Come to Take You Home," that had been recorded by The Isaacs. My rendition of the song was a "train wreck"; I forgot a lot of the words and by the time it was over, I was quite embarrassed. I felt like crawling under something. Hoping to redeem myself, I introduced a new song that I had just written entitled "Through the Fire."

We had sung it only a few times, but I was confident that my son Jason could pull it off. He worked great under pressure. Although we were unsure of the lyrics and even the melody of the new song "Through the Fire," the presence of the Lord came down. It was a very special moment; that night I was reassured that there was something extraordinary about this song.

After the debut of the new song, several artists and producers approached me. Some of the artists were interested in recording the song, while some producers wanted to put it on hold for one of their artists to record. I felt honored, yet very humbled, by all the interest.

However, I knew that this song was a gift given to me from God for us to use as a ministry tool to offer comfort to the weary and the hurting. It proved to be just that.

When we released the song as a radio single in the year 2000, it reached the number one position in only three months, and it stayed there for three consecutive months: May, June, and July of 2000.

An amazing flood of interest in the song was soon to follow, along with acclaim and awards.

"Through The Fire" was named the *Singing News* # 1 Song of the Year in all of southern gospel music.

It earned the BMI Airplay Award at the 2001 BMI Christian Music Awards.

It won the Dove Award at the 36th Annual GMA Music Awards for Traditional Gospel Recorded Song of The Year; that recording featured The Crabb Family and Donnie McClurkin. That same year it was nominated at the GMA Music Awards as overall song of the year.

The song won the Dove Award at the 37th Annual GMA Music Awards for Southern Gospel Recorded Song of the Year; that recording featured The Crabb Family and The Brooklyn Tabernacle Choir.

"Through The Fire" was also featured on the album *Glory Train* by Randy Travis, which in 2007 was named Best Southern, Country, or Blue Grass Album at the 49th Annual Grammy Awards.

"Through the Fire" was featured on the Grammy-winning album: *Jason Crabb* by Jason Crabb. In 2010, that album was named Best Southern, Country or Blue Grass album at the 52nd Annual Grammy Awards.

In addition, the song was performed on the Gaither Homecoming series, *New Orleans Homecoming* recorded in New Orleans, Louisiana. Bill Gaither later shared with me that he thought the song was one of the highlights of the evening.

I will never forget the night of the 34th Annual Dove Awards, which was held on April 10, 2003, in Nashville, Tennessee, at the Sommet Center (Currently Bridgestone Arena). The Crabb Family performed "Through the Fire" to a crowd of several thousand people from all types of Christian music backgrounds. As the Who's Who of Gospel Music listened, the presence of the Lord came down. Everyone in the building was on his or her feet. I can't explain the joy I felt as a writer as I watched a multitude of people wiping tears from their eyes and praising God.

On May 2, 2010, "Through the Fire" was featured on the *Song of a Lifetime* video recorded at the First Baptist Church of Atlanta in Atlanta, Georgia. Dr. Charles Stanley, who serves as pastor, delivered the opening remarks of the evening. Daniel Crews performed "Through the Fire" along with the First Baptist Church choir and orchestra. It was a very special evening.

This song has defied gospel music boundaries as it has been performed around the world and in various styles by a variety of artist ranging from Grammy-winning Brooklyn Tabernacle Choir to Country Music Association male vocalist winner Randy Travis.

This song has taken quite a journey in the past decade, receiving a lot of accolades and acclaim, but the real treasures are the stories of people that have been touched and changed. The stories that follow put the words of this God-given song into perspective.

What you will read in these pages is not just about a song, "Through the Fire" as presented on a performance stage, but more importantly, how its message has impacted the lives of every day people.

Chapter 1

He Will Take You through the Fire Again

In January 2009, my wife and I were at a restaurant in Corinth, Mississippi, visiting with some friends who were passing through on their way home to Virginia. What a beautiful family. Cas and Marcia Horton's oldest is a son named Levi, and he is absolutely a prince of a child. His sisters, Farris and Rachel, look and act like little movie stars. Shirley Temple comes to my mind every time I see them. All three children are filled with personality.

After about an hour and a half of good food and visitation—and of course a few snapshots—we followed them out to their motor home. Cas was excited about a recording that his son had done the night before and wanted us to listen to it. I will never forget putting those headphones on and listening to that little 10-year-old guy sing a song that I had written—"Through the Fire."

I became very emotional by what I heard. Levi sang every word of that song with such feeling. It was as if he knew exactly what he was singing about. After conversing with this family for a while, it was easy to see why this particular song meant so much to this young man, for his whole life seemed to be a journey "through the fire."

When I think of the Horton family, I think of the Norman Rockwell pictures. Here you have this sweet couple with strong faith in God raising their three children in the community where they grew up themselves.

Both sets of grandparents are retired and live nearby, and their whole lives revolve around their grandkids. The area in which they live is one of the most beautiful places in the United States. As a matter of fact, it is only about fifty miles away from Mount Airy, North Carolina—the little mountain town that inspired *The Andy Griffith Show* and *Mayberry R.F.D.*

Cas and Marcia met and married while in their late teens. It seemed to be divine intervention that brought them together. Marcia first met Cas in a store parking lot where she had been stranded with a girlfriend when Marcia's car overheated. Cas and another young man, known to Marcia, stopped to help fix the car's radiator problem. Marcia said that when she encountered Cas her response was, "Oh, my!"

She previously had seen him several times and thought that he was handsome, but she didn't think he had noticed her. As the two young men were departing after helping the stranded girls to get on their way, Cas asked Marcia if he could meet her for lunch the next day.

Marcia's thought, "Oh, sure," thinking that he wouldn't even show up, but he did. While having lunch, he asked her out on a date. For the next two months they saw each other every night. It was during that time that Cas proposed, and at the end of the two months they got married.

The couple was married in Galax, Virginia, in the church that Marcia had attended most of her life. The wedding was absolutely beautiful, and Cas could not take his eyes off his stunning bride as she marched down the aisle. For their honeymoon they drove to Gatlinburg, Tennessee, about four hours away. The new Horton family decided to live in Austinville, Virginia, where Cas had grown up.

At the time they were married, Cas was doing construction work and Marcia was getting into hair styling. She later obtained her cosmetology license and began working for a local hair salon near Hillsville, Virginia.

As the years passed, they found themselves being drawn back to their Christian upbringing. One Sunday morning in October 1996, in a little country church, they walked to the altar together and rededicated their lives to Christ.

About a year later, Cas was riding home from church with a friend, when the friend turned to him and said, "I feel like the Lord wants me to ask you something." Without hesitation he asked, "Are you going to preach God's word or not?" Cas was blown away because he had recently been struggling with his feelings on this question. To him, this was just the confirmation he needed to go forward with what he felt God had called him to do. He began his ministry in November 1997.

In the first year he ministered in his home church under the direction and leadership of his pastor. The following year was a very exciting time in their lives. Their ministry had begun to branch out; they were traveling around conducting revivals.

On September 17, 1998, the couple was blessed with a baby boy. They named him Castus Levi Horton. He weighed seven pounds fourteen ounces. The parents said that they would never forget the words when the nurse smiled and said, "He's perfect."

Family and friends came to share this special occasion. Grandparents stood around the bed retelling the stories of when their babies were born. One of them said that Levi looked like his mom; another said he looked identical to his dad. It was an atmosphere filled with love and joy.

Two months later, at their home church and in the presence of friends and family, Baby Levi was dedicated to God by their pastor. By the time he was six months old he was saying "Daddy;" before he was ten months old he was walking. For the first year and a half it seemed that one could literally watch him grow. Every day he was learning new things.

Everything seemed to be perfect for the first eighteen months. But then Levi began having problems with his stomach. Within two weeks time, several trips were made to the doctor without finding the problem. On March 26, 2000, Levi's condition worsened. His joints became stiff and he became very weak and tired, to the point where he did not want to play or eat. Marcia and Cas knew something was definitely wrong.

They decided to take Levi immediately to another doctor, a long-time family physician. Mom and Dad were by his side with Mom holding his Winnie the Pooh for him. The doctor took one look at him and realized there was a serious problem. The doctor suggested that Levi be given a CT scan immediately. He was sedated so that he would lie still as the machine obtained images.

As the scan was conducted, the family noticed that an unusual number of nurses and technicians had gathered in the room to look at the video screen. There was a stunned silence as they stared at the screen.

Marcia and Cas knew something was terribly wrong. They began to pray, "God, please let our baby be okay."

When the scan was completed, the family was sent to another room to wait. After what seemed like an eternity, the doctor burst through the door and said, "I wish I had better news for you folks, but your son has a brain tumor, and it is huge. We have to get him to another hospital fast!"

Marcia recalled feeling shock and disbelief when she heard the horrible report. "The mental pain was almost more than we could bear," she said. She and Cas embraced and collapsed into each other's arms as their world came crashing in around them. Their son lay sleeping with no clue how sick he was. All they could do was cry and scream, "Why God, why?"

To Marcia, the ride in the ambulance to Winston Salem, North Carolina, was a blur. It was dark outside when they arrived. They felt as if they were in a hellish nightmare from which they could not wake up. It was a time when one feels alone even in the midst of loving family and friends. Over and over Cas would kiss Levi and assure him, "Daddy is here."

When they arrived, Levi was immediately taken to the MRI room. It was like a repeat of the CT scan, as he lay unconscious through another test. After the test, Levi was put in another room with three babies that were terminally ill. Marcia recalls thinking, "My baby does not belong in here." Both grandpas took turns holding Little Levi throughout the night.

The neurosurgeon scheduled surgery for the next morning. A shunt was to be implanted to reduce pressure on Levi's brain. During the operation, the surgeon decided to do more extensive exploratory surgery, removing a large portion of Levi's skull. However, to the surgeon's disappointment, he discovered that nothing could be done surgically to remove the tumor at that time because of its size.

Several hours passed before Levi was out of surgery. When he was rolled into the hallway, the Hortons did not recognize their own child. His shaven head was severely swollen, with bandages covering most of one side. He could not move his entire left side. Little Levi had suffered a stroke that would later prove devastating by leaving his left arm paralyzed. He began to have one seizure after another.

It was difficult for them to understand how their child, who was so vibrant and full of life just two weeks before, was now fighting for his life. The doctors could not determine whether the paralysis would be permanent. The Hortons had never been in a valley this low; at times it felt as if God had forsaken them. The faith that Levi's father had preached about so many times before was now being severely put to the test.

Seventy-two grueling weeks of chemotherapy treatments soon began. The plan was to shrink the tumor down to a size that was operable. Life as the Hortons knew it would never be the same. Before the horrible tumor, Little Levi's life was filled with fun times as Mom and Dad were constantly teaching him new things and playing games with him. He would anxiously wait for Dad to come home from work so they could wrestle on the floor. Now, those fun days were replaced with numerous doctor visits and many needles.

Monday was the day blood was drawn to get a blood count; Tuesday was chemotherapy; Wednesday and Thursday were physical therapy and occupational therapy days. Finally, a break from all the doctor's visits would come on Friday and the family would get to spend the day at home. However, Levi's "Fridays," as he once knew them, were gone. The family tried desperately to create a semblance of normalcy for the sake of their son whom they loved so deeply, but after all the needles and tests he had endured through the week, his weak and frail body just simply needed to rest.

While Levi weighed twenty-seven pounds before his sickness, his weight fell to sixteen pounds during his treatments. He was so tiny; he looked like a skeleton. He could not lift his head or sit up alone. It was very difficult for him to eat because the chemo treatments made him nauseated and very sick. For the next eight months he was kept alive by drinking a supplement drink. That, along with the grace of God, was all that kept him alive. Yet through it all, the "little trooper" never complained.

Levi's second surgery was on January 18, 2001. The tumor was down to an operable size—the size of a golf ball. His doctor felt very confident. Levi was in surgery for about eight hours. When he came out of recovery, the first two things he asked for were his mommy and his sippy cup; that was music to their ears. The final report was that the doctors were ninety-nine percent sure they had removed the entire tumor. What a blessing! What a relief! God truly had answered many of the family's prayers.

From the time Levi learned to walk, all he ever wanted to do was preach like his daddy. Preaching and singing became a big part of his life, especially since his dad was a traveling evangelist. Everywhere they would go, Little Levi would sing and preach. People were amazed and blessed by his strong spirit.

On September 9, 2001, Cas Horton became pastor of Galax First Assembly of God. At this time, things were going great for the Hortons. The church began to grow, and Levi's health was very good. Everything seemed to get back to normal, except for the intermittent MRIs and check-ups.

Almost three years passed by and Levi was doing great. In November 2003 he became a big brother to Farris Rebekah, who weighed eight pounds fourteen and one-half ounces. It was going to be tough being a big brother, but Levi was determined to do a great job. He fell in love with his baby sister as soon as she was born. They were such a blessing to each other.

When the time came for Levi to start school, his parents enrolled him in a private Christian school. He had to wear a necktie to school every day, which was right up his alley, since he loved dressing like a preacher.

Having been in school three months, Levi was doing great. It was time for another MRI. On November 15, 2004, Marcia and Cas received news they had hoped and prayed they would never hear. The doctors informed them that the tumor was back with a vengeance. Marcia and Cas felt the walls caving in around them once again as their spirits tried to digest this horrible report. They were devastated and heartbroken, but they tried hard not to show their feelings in front of their son. They did not want him to be scared by their reaction to the news.

As they drove down the road on their way home from the hospital, they heard a sweet little voice coming from the back seat, singing one of his favorite songs—"Through the Fire." Levi sang,

> He never promised the cross would not be heavy, and the hill would
> not be hard to climb.

He never offered our victories without fighting, but he said help
would always come in time.

Just remember when you're standing in the valley of decision and
the adversary says give in.

Just hold on, our God will show up, and he will take you through
the fire again!

The parents' cries quickly became shouts of praise as they realized
their five-year-old son was ministering to them. His mother said the
song seemed to reach out to them like the comforting arms of God, and
hold them tight through countless days. They realized the comfort that
Levi had given them that day was a special gift from God.

For the next six months, Levi was put on a different kind of
chemotherapy, which was in the form of a pill. When they went to
the pharmacy to pick up the prescription, they were informed that the
insurance would not cover the cost. The prescription called for three
pills a day for forty-two days at the cost of $5,000. Marcia responded,
"He has to have them; what are we going to do?"

The pharmacist gave them a few pills to get them started. The
Hortons left the drug store very distraught and unsure as to how they
were going to afford this medication. If need be, they were willing to
sell whatever they had to make sure that their son was able to get his
medication. When word got out in the community about the high
cost of the medication, people showed their love and support as they
came forward with a willingness to help. Several people went as far as to
tell the Hortons not to worry, that they would make sure Levi got his
medication. Isn't it amazing how a crisis brings people together?

Because of Levi's previous stroke it was very difficult for him to
swallow the large pills—three pills every morning. Cas or Marcia had to
literally push the pill down their son's throat by finger because he could
not swallow them on his own without vomiting. Those were some very
hard times, but Levi would always say, "It's okay, Mommy, I know I have
to take them." He was always so brave and strong. Mom and Dad would
give him the medicine and then go into another room and cry.

After six months of chemo, an MRI was taken, and the results were
not good. The tumor had increased in size instead of decreasing. Levi

was immediately scheduled for his third craniotomy (cutting out and putting back a part of the skull during surgery). The already distraught family had a little less than two weeks to prepare for their son's next surgery. They took Levi and his sister to the beach on a short vacation, hoping to get him to focus his attention on something pleasant rather than on the grueling surgery he was facing. He played and tried to have fun, but his parents could see that he was growing weaker and weaker. It was so painful for them to watch their child's health deteriorate so quickly.

The day of the surgery seemed to come quickly—June 25, 2005. A caravan of friends and family followed them to the hospital. Levi watched a movie in the van on the way there. He seemed very calm and very brave. He was admitted into the hospital, and Marcia and Cas stayed with him for as long as they were permitted.

As a kind gentleman took him away for surgery, Mom and Dad kept reminding Levi of how much they loved him. They reassured him that they would be waiting for him, and it would be over soon. Their hearts were crushed as they heard Levi crying for them all the way down the hall. Mom stated, "I got the most sickening feeling that something was terribly wrong. I felt the urgency to go after him, to get him and take him back home where it was safe." She said, "The feeling of dread and despair surrounded us. Waves of helplessness and fear swept over us to the point we felt we would drown. Our anguish was indescribable; we felt somehow we had let him down."

After about eight agonizing hours of waiting and praying, the surgery was finally over. The doctors came out to tell the Horton family that their son had come through the surgery, but that they had been unable to remove the entire tumor because of its location. The next few words the family heard pierced their hearts like a dagger. The doctor said, "Levi has awakened from surgery, but he cannot see; he is blind." The parents were in total shock as they tried to come to grips with the reality of their son being blind. This God-fearing family didn't want to question God's plan for Levi, yet they couldn't help but ask, "Hasn't this child already endured enough pain to last a lifetime?"

A little while later, the family was told that Levi was ready for them to visit him. Their pain and agony were almost unbearable. How were they supposed to act? What were they going to say? Questions with no answers!

No one around them could hold back the tears. Family and friends were in utter disbelief. As Marcia and Cas walked into Levi's room, they saw a look of terror on their son's face as he cried out, his little hands groping the darkness. At this moment, he desperately needed to feel the loving arms of his parents holding him close and telling him that everything was going to be all right. How many times in the past had those loving arms and soothing voices comforted him and helped drive away his fears?

All the while Levi was crying for his parents, they were rushing to get to him; the few steps separating them and their son felt like a mile. Their only thoughts were, "We've got to get to him and hold him close. He can't see us, but he can feel our love." After they finally reached him, they kept echoing the words: "We will never leave you." (Doesn't that sound familiar?)

Directly over Levi's head a bright light was shining, but though he was staring straight into it, he could see nothing. His eyes were wide open, searching and searching for any sign of light. All this time he was screaming, "Mommy, I'm in a dungeon, and I can't get out! They won't let me out! Mommy there's something on my eyes; they won't take it off! It's dark, Mommy; I'm in a dungeon!"

During those moments the questions kept flooding their minds: "Where is God? Why did this happen? How did God let this happen?" (More unanswered questions.)

All the while Levi was still crying, "I'm in a dark hole, and they won't let me out." Their minds were in turmoil and their hearts were crushed as they searched for words to comfort their son. It was the most horrible thing they had ever faced.

Having previously lost the use of his left arm due to a stroke, now, at age seven, Levi had to learn how to function totally blind.

I remember the first time that I met the Horton family. It was April 28, 2006. I was booked for a revival at the Galax First Assembly of God; Cas Horton was the pastor. I was aware of all that Levi and his family had gone through. I had spoken with them on the phone and had prayed many prayers for them, but had never met them personally.

When I first spoke with Levi, I was amazed by his in-depth knowledge of God and his spirituality. He was about eight years old at the time. During the service, he would sing and pray, and as I preached, he would cling onto every word. Often his response was, "Amen, preach it brother." He was deeper in the things of God than many thirty-year-old Christians. He may be legally blind, but he sees a whole lot more than most people do.

I remember a story his mother told about an experience Levi had at school. After she had picked him up from school one afternoon he said, "I don't know why you make me go to that place. They won't let me sing, pray, or preach." Even though Levi felt certain restraints upon his ministry at school, the fact remains that many of the students and even some of the teachers were asking Levi to pray for certain situations in their lives.

It would be difficult for anyone to understand why this family has had to go through such trying times. But the heat of the fire has only produced pure gold. They are stronger than ever in their faith. I feel confident that this experience of Levi having gone through the fire has helped shape and mold him into becoming the singer, the preacher, the prayer warrior, and the solid Christian he is today.

In August 2006, when I was at Galax First Assembly of God to conduct another revival, I was able to spend more time with the Horton family. One night after church, Levi asked if I wanted to see his pulpit. His grandfather had bought a pulpit at a yard sale and had cut it down to his grandson's size. I said, "Sure, I would like to see it."

He said, "Follow me." I followed him to the top of the stairs. The walk up the stairs was very dark, and I had to be careful not to stumble. However, Levi was as sure-footed as a mountain goat as he climbed to the top of the stairs, turned and continued to walk in a hallway.

I recall at one point calling out, "Levi, I can't see where I'm going."

His reply was, "Just follow the thumps." As he snapped his fingers, I walked in the darkness following the snaps.

Then it dawned on me: "We walk by faith, not by sight." It was scary. I felt like any minute I might be stepping into a hole, yet my trust was totally in that snap. When I got to where he was, he reached and turned the light on in the room, and there it was, a miniature pulpit. He told me there were times when he would feel a burning message that he just had to preach and his grandmother would often be his audience.

In late summer of 2008, Levi went for a checkup. He had been suffering from severe headaches and pain in his back. The report from the MRI was devastating. Levi's parents were told that something very unusual had developed which presented some serious problems. The tumor had seeded from his brain steam all the way down his spine, into his spinal fluid, and down to his tailbone. The physician explained that they could try chemo treatments, but since these treatments had not worked on the original tumor, it was very unlikely that they would work on these many seed tumors.

Levi's childlike response to the report was, "I don't want to hear what that doctor said, and he can just go to Alaska as far as I'm concerned."

Shortly after the bad report, my son, Aaron, and his wife, Amanda were conducting a revival at the church where Levi's dad pastored in Galax, Virginia. One night, in the service, Aaron prayed for Levi. It was a very special moment. Levi said that as Aaron was praying for him, it felt like electricity running all the way down his back. Since that night his severe headaches and back pain have been gone.

In August 2009, Pastor Horton asked if I would come and preach a revival at their church. One night during the revival, I was privileged to sing "Through the Fire" with my buddy, Levi Horton. I can't explain the feeling I experienced as I just stepped back and let him sing. It was those same words that he had sung to his parents five years earlier after they had received a horrible report from one of his MRIs. There he was, five years later, still going through the fire, still trusting in the Lord, and still singing praises unto the Lord.

I don't know what God has in store for that little guy, but I know it's something great. He has walked through the fire, alongside his parents, most of his life. I have never met a thirteen-year-old child with such strong faith. He has come to know God in a very personal way. His entire life has been and continues to be a living testimony to the masses of how they, too, if they put their trust in God, can walk through the fiery trials of life.

I recall reading and preaching messages about Job, and how while going through his "furnace of affliction" he said, "Though he slay me, yet will I trust him . . ." Job 13:15 (NKJV). Job didn't understand what was going on. Yet, in the midst of all the turmoil and the many, many questions with no answers, he declared that he would still trust in God.

That's the kind of relationship Levi has with his God. He never complains about his handicaps and never sings the old "Woe Is Me" song. He just loves life and God. This young man puts most of us to shame. While we sit around complaining about our little mishaps, this brave little soldier is "facing the giant" on a daily basis. It can be said without a doubt that Levi has truly been "through the fire" and has come forth as *pure gold*.

Chapter 2

So Many Times I've Questioned

Cathy and Eddie met at a tent revival in Bowling Green, Kentucky, in 1974. The couple dated for three years before they were married. Their first child was a boy, Steven. A year later they were blessed with a little girl, Autumn. Both children were dedicated to the Lord in a special ceremony shortly after they were born.

Steven was the well-mannered, respectful, and obedient child who always said "Yes, ma'am" and "No, sir." He excelled in everything he did, including sports and academics. Autumn, however, was a different story. Cathy's philosophy was that every parent needs to have one of each—a boy and a girl: one to keep you sane and one to keep you on your knees, close to God.

According to Cathy, Autumn was the one that kept them on their knees and close to God, especially in her childhood years. She was known for having lots and lots of energy. If she were a child living in today's society, the teachers would have possibly tried to persuade the McGuffey's to put her on medication. She was extremely hyper and loved to make up stories—what young child doesn't, right? Yet her stories were sometimes a little far-fetched.

When Autumn was in the third grade, her mom received a letter from her guidance counselor informing her that she needed to meet with them to discuss a very important matter. The next day she met with the counselor. The counselor commenced to tell Cathy that Autumn had told her that her mom had beaten her, and she even showed the counselor a bruise on her arm. The counselor knew the McGuffey family, and she did not feel the allegation was legitimate. However, since the accusations were made, she was legally obligated to report the incident.

At first they were devastated—to say the least. Later, they found humor in it—very much later. Autumn was always doing things to get attention—no matter if it was good or bad. After the counselor and Autumn's mom had discussed the matter privately, the counselor then brought Autumn into the room. She spoke with her about why her mom was there and asked Autumn, "Is it true that your mother beats you?"

She looked at the counselor and said, "No, ma'am, I lied."

The counselor then asked Autumn why she had lied, but she was unable to give her an answer. In front of the counselor, Cathy looked at Autumn and said, "No, I have never beaten you, but when I get you home today I'm going to."

She didn't beat her, but she did use some extreme disciplinary action on her for telling such lies.

Just a few weeks before the bruise incident, the teacher had called Cathy to discuss Autumn's behavior in class. The child had gotten down on her hands and knees and crawled over two isles to talk to her friend—this was after the teacher had separated both children for talking.

These are the words of a mother who raised an extremely hyper and disobedient child:

> Never give up. My child was rebellious, would not listen, lied, back-talked, angered easily, and exaggerated things. She would often trash her room by scattering toys all over the floor and throwing clothes out of her closet or chest. Autumn's behavior was very exhausting. In those days we didn't know what it was like to enjoy a moment of peace and quiet in our home, Yet, Thank God, there is hope! Prayer does change things. Sometimes it may take many years of constant love, encouragement, patience, discipline and prayer. All of these ingredients mentioned paid off.

At a young age Autumn accepted Jesus Christ as her Savior. Shortly thereafter, Eddie and Cathy began to see major changes take place in their daughter.

The McGuffey children loved to go to church. It was never a question of, "Are you going to church today?" It was just what the family did; it was a major part of their lives. Family-prayer time was a common practice in their home. The Bible was read to the children when they were young.

One night both of the children approached their mom and said, "We have been talking, and we think we would get a lot more out of the Bible if we read it ourselves and had our own devotions." She knew at that moment that her children were growing up, and that they were developing their own relationship with Christ.

One particular Sunday their pastor's wife, Shirley, gave each of the students in her class a journal. She shared with them that sometimes it is hard to express your feelings with someone else, so just write down your feelings in the journal as a prayer and tell Jesus the things you are feeling and experiencing in your life. That was the beginning of many journal entries for Autumn. The journal has since become a priceless treasure.

When Autumn was sixteen, Cathy said that she noticed a knot on the right side of her daughter's neck. She was immediately taken to the doctor, and from there Autumn was sent to the hospital for some additional tests. The doctor called Cathy into a separate room and pointed out to her the results of the X-ray. A mass was wrapped around the main vein in Autumn's neck. The doctor said that it could be very serious but encouraged them to remain positive. He scheduled the surgery, and family and friends began to pray.

On the day of the surgery, the waiting room was packed with family and friends. The wait seemed like an eternity. When the doctor came out, he had a look of relief on his face as he informed them that it was not cancer, and at those words everyone breathed a sigh of relief. It was a bronchial cleft cyst. The infection had gotten so intense that it had consumed the entire center of the cyst. The doctor removed it but said that he could not guarantee that another one would not return.

Everyone began to celebrate and thank God for the good news. Autumn recovered quite quickly from the surgery.

Autumn loved people. She had learned to channel that high energy of hers into loving people. She was always reaching out and constantly making new friends. The status of the person didn't matter; rich or poor, she treated everyone the same.

She loved working with the teens at church and singing in the church choir. She had also gotten involved in the Big Brothers and Big Sisters program and had adopted a little sister named Tiosha. Autumn became a very positive figure in her life. Cathy stated that when she attended Tiosha's graduation in 2009, Tiosha told her that Autumn had helped to make that day possible.

Steve and Autumn loved going to Christian youth events such as Winter Fest! It was one the highlights of their lives. Winter Fest is an event where hundreds of young people come together in one place to worship Christ and to be spiritually refueled. Every year they would return home recharged and full of spiritual zeal.

Autumn was by nature a planner and organizer, and she had typed out her agenda and goals for her entire life. One goal was to graduate from Western Kentucky University. She also wanted to marry a Christian man, have a family, and have a home that was just big enough to suit their needs—nothing fancy. She was determined to accomplish all these goals by 2011.

Autumn began dating Jonathan (Jay) Redmond, a great Christian young man from their church. It wasn't long before they had fallen in love, and he asked Eddie and Cathy for their daughter's hand in marriage. The parents said yes to the marriage, but with one stipulation: Their daughter had to finish her last year of college. Autumn and Jay agreed, and right away, they began searching for a home. They closed on the home a few weeks before they were married.

It was a bittersweet time in the lives of the McGuffey family.

Bitter because their little girl was being transformed into a young lady right before their eyes. Within a few days her bedroom would be empty, and she would be in a home of her own. Sweet because she had met such a wonderful young man who would take very good care of their daughter, and it would be as if they were gaining another son.

The parents began planning for the wedding that would take place in May 2001. Autumn wanted a big wedding with the colors of a spring bouquet, and she chose periwinkle blue to be her main color. Autumn had requested that her mom write a song for her to sing to Jay at their wedding. It was to be a big surprise for him.

It was one month before the wedding, and Cathy just couldn't seem to get inspired to write. No matter how hard she tried, nothing would come. Eddie and Cathy decided to go ahead and schedule their vacation and go to a beach in South Carolina. They thought that getting away from the hustle and bustle of life, sitting on the beach, looking out across the vast ocean, and listening to the waves softly beating against the shore would bring the inspiration needed for the wedding song.

On the second day of her parent's vacation Autumn called, "Mom, have you written the song yet?" On the third day she called, and on the fourth. Each day the answer was, "No." The anxious bride was getting nervous because the wedding was getting close and still no wedding song. Finally on the fourth day, the inspiration came and the lyrics and tune began to flow, and Cathy began to write the love song that Autumn sang to her beloved on their wedding day.

Cathy was concerned whether her mother would be able to attend her granddaughter's wedding, since she had suffered a severe stroke that had left her unable to use the right side of her body. Cathy and her mother were very close, and Autumn absolutely adored her grandmother. She called her "Granny." When the stroke first occurred, Autumn's grandmother was unable to eat, talk, or walk, but thank God, by the time the wedding came around, she had improved to the point where she was able to attend.

The wedding party was made up of five bridesmaids and five groomsmen. There was barely enough room to sit as family and friends gathered to help celebrate this joyous occasion. The church was decorated with beautiful flower arrangements and white columns overflowing with ivy and spring flowers. Yet, all this beauty paled in comparison to the beautiful bride. Autumn was gorgeous as she walked down the aisle. As she serenaded her groom, Jay wept softly. Her dream had come true, and she had gotten her storybook wedding.

When November rolled around, there was more excitement added to the new Redman Family. One Wednesday night at church Autumn broke the news to her mother that she was going to be a grandmother. The soon-to-be grandmother was thrilled, but Autumn was upset because this unexpected event was not supposed to be on her agenda at this point in her life. She still needed to finish her internship and get her degree at WKU. The pregnancy, however, was soon accepted as part of the God's divine plan for their lives. Each day became more exciting as the family anxiously awaited the arrival of their special little gift from God.

The couple decided that when the ultra-sound was performed, they wanted to find out whether they were having a boy or a girl. They invited nearly the whole neighborhood to help celebrate this glorious occasion, but they were disappointed when the doctor was unable to determine the baby's gender. Later, they had another ultra-sound performed, but the news was the same, so they decided they would just have to be patient and wait.

Autumn and Jay loved Christian music; they especially enjoyed attending the Dove Awards. The year 2002 was no different. Autumn called her mom at work with such an excitement in her voice: "Mom, I have found the most perfect dress at Dillard's! It is periwinkle blue, and Mom, I look so skinny!" She loved to dress up on this special night out with her husband, and since she was pregnant, this dress would be perfect.

She continued: "One catch, Mom, I do not have the money to pay for the dress! It's on sale though, and I will pay you back!" Of course Mom bought the dress for her daughter, even though it was the most she had ever paid for a dress. Cathy said that it was a dress that she would never forget.

About eight months into the pregnancy, Autumn began experiencing pain in her back and legs. She also had some pain in her mouth. Everyone thought that the back and leg pains were part of the last days of pregnancy due to the weight of the baby, and the pain was normal. Autumn had gotten dental braces about a year earlier, so she thought the braces were causing the pain in her mouth. Just to make sure that the braces were the problem, she made an appointment with the orthodontist.

During that time everyone was devastated because Autumn's grandmother had suffered a second stroke, and the family knew that it was just a matter of time before she would be taken away from them. Autumn would sit in the hospital room at the foot of her granny's bed until late in the evening. The night before her grandmother passed, Autumn did not want to leave, but Cathy finally convinced her daughter that she and the baby she was carrying needed rest. Early the next morning "Granny" fell asleep in this world and woke up in the presence of the Lord.

Jay had written a poem that the family wanted him to read at the funeral; he loved Granny Miller like his own grandmother. He didn't think that he could get through the reading of the poem, so Autumn said, "I will do it." It was a bittersweet time for the family. They had no doubt that their precious loved one was in the presence of the Lord, yet they were not ready to let her go. At the end of funeral, Cathy held her daughter in her arms as she wept and said, "Granny will never get to hold our baby, and she will not get to watch her grow up."

Eddie and Cathy had already scheduled a vacation and had purchased plane tickets, and it just so happened they were to fly out the week after her mother's funeral. Several loved ones convinced them that they should go ahead with their plans because they needed to get away. Autumn encouraged her mom to get away and try to get some rest.

A few days before they left, Autumn sent her mother a beautiful flower: a Smiley Face Mum. Attached to the mum were long eyelashes, hair bows, and on its face, the biggest smile. With the mum was a card that read, "from Autumn and Jay." Autumn was so worried about her mom that she would call her supervisor to check on her mother to make sure that she was okay. She would email her, sometimes two or three times a day, to check in to see how she was doing. Even though Autumn was grieving over her grandmother's passing, her only concern at this time seemed to be about her mom.

Autumn insisted on driving her parents to the airport to catch their flight. They laughed just about all the way to the airport. Autumn shared with them that she had been praying to the Lord, asking that He would not punish her for all the mean things she had done while she was growing up. She said she hoped her child would be different and treat her better. Once again they all burst into laughter.

Before parting ways at the airport Autumn promised that if she went into labor early or anything changed that she would call her parents, and they would be on the first flight back.

Two days later, Monday evening, she called and said, "Mom, I am at the emergency room, and Jay is with me. I was in so much pain that we came to make sure everything was okay with the baby." She continued, "The doctor said that the baby is lying on the sciatic nerve, and that is what's causing the pain. He is giving me something to help alleviate the pain and told me to soak and take long warm baths. The baby and I are okay."

After much talking, she convinced her parents to finish their vacation. They called and checked on her every day, and she seemed to feel better each day.

One night while on vacation Cathy had a dream. In the dream there were hundreds of people gathered in a building—some she knew and some she didn't. She first saw her son's wife, Karen, and then she saw a casket. Cathy woke up with great fear and immediately began praying for God's protection upon their son.

When the vacation was over, and Autumn picked her parents up at the airport, she seemed to be doing great. She and Jay had planned a big get-together that night at their new home and wanted to cook a nice meal for her parents, her brother and his wife, and a few close friends.

As everyone began to arrive for the evening, the dream that Cathy had experienced weighed heavily on her mind. She shared it with Autumn, especially since it involved her brother. They were more than just mother and daughter; they were best of friends.

When Steven and Karen arrived, Cathy gave Steven the biggest hug ever; she was so happy to see him come through the door. He had no idea why his mother was being so clingy. They had a wonderful dinner and played the Uno Attack card game until midnight. It was a great family night; priceless memories were made.

The next day was Sunday. Autumn woke up with her mouth hurting so bad that she could hardly eat anything, and her entire body was in pain. Jay brought her to her parent's home. Cathy made her potato soup; she was able to eat a bowl of it. Her mom tried to make her daughter as comfortable as she could. Autumn slept on and off the rest of the evening. After Jay returned from church, he took his wife back to their home.

June 5, 2002, was a Monday, and what seemed to be just another day at work, but it turned into a day that Cathy said she would never forget. Autumn—now eight and a half months into her pregnancy—called her mother at work a little after 7:00 a. m. She had awakened in a pool of blood. Jay had left for work already, so she had called him to come back home. She then called the doctor, who told her to come directly to his office because she was in premature labor. That doctor also alerted Autumn's pediatrician and asked if he could meet them at the hospital because he thought that she was in labor. All the while trying to soothe and calm her daughter, Cathy assured her that what was happening was not uncommon.

By this time, Cathy was very concerned and called her husband to let him know. She then asked a friend to please send out emails and ask people to pray that all would be okay, and for God's protection upon Autumn and the baby. In the meantime, Jay had called his parents, who lived out of town, and told them to be praying.

As soon as the doctor hooked up the baby monitor, he could see that the baby was in distress and ordered an emergency C-section. He called the hospital and told them that Autumn was on her way. The doctor's main concern was to save the baby. Though Jay and his wife had taken Lamaze classes and had hoped for a natural childbirth, nothing prepared them for what was about to happen.

When Autumn arrived at the hospital, the nurses immediately hooked her up to an IV. They also hooked up heart monitors for both her and the baby. Autumn's blood pressure kept shooting up, and the family tried to calm her down by making her laugh. Autumn said, "Mom, can we just pray right now, together?" The mother and daughter began to pray. When the baby's doctor arrived, they quickly took Autumn into surgery. Jay was not allowed to go into delivery, but Autumn assured him that she felt a sense of peace that the Lord would be with her.

Autumn's doctor said to give them about fifteen minutes, and if they heard the music, they would know that the baby was fine. If they didn't, they should keep praying. Every minute seemed like an eternity. After thirty minutes had passed, everyone was getting really concerned. Then all of a sudden they heard the most beautiful music—the cry of a tiny baby. It was such a beautiful sound.

About ten minutes later the nurse brought out a beautiful baby girl. Cathy stated that it would be difficult to express in words the relief and joy they all felt at that moment, especially Jay. She said that he was as proud as any father she had ever seen. Everyone was wiping away tears of joy and thanking God at that moment. What a roller coaster ride they had been on.

The baby looked perfect! Flashes of light filled the room as cameras were going off left and right. Jay and Autumn named her Kaley Nicole Redmond. The waiting room was filled with family and friends all wanting to share in this joyous occasion.

The doctor came out later and informed the family that Autumn had lost fifty percent of her blood during the surgery, and they could not get the bleeding to stop. They were continuously giving her blood. He was asked if he thought it was cancer, and he said "No." He thought it was toxemia (toxic substances in the blood), but they wanted to be certain, so they were calling in an oncologist.

The doctor had barely left when he returned with the specialist. The oncologist stated that Autumn had acute leukemia. Everyone was in shock. Eddie and Cathy thought that their daughter was healthy, and what she had been experiencing was only the side effects of a normal pregnancy. Her mouth had been hurting and sore, but they had attributed that to her braces. They later learned that the sore mouth and all the other symptoms were side effects of the acute leukemia. The grandparents thought that the emotional roller-coaster ride was finally over after their grandchild was born, but it now seemed to have just begun.

There were so many questions: "How could the doctor have missed this? Why did her blood work not reveal the disease?" In times such as this, people often look for someone to blame, but there was no one to blame. The doctor said that apparently the disease was dormant, and the pregnancy brought it out full scale. Afraid that such bad news would cause Autumn to lose her will to fight, the family decided to ask the doctor if he could hold-off on telling her the results of the last tests until she was stronger. After all, she had not even held her baby yet.

The next day was when the doctor was to tell Autumn the results of the tests. The pastor of their home church, Stephen, and his wife, Shirley, along with several close friends and family had gathered in Autumn's room to support her and Jay—she had to know that something was terribly wrong. The oncologist came in and shared with her that she had acute leukemia. Everyone was fighting to hold back the tears as Autumn looked at the doctor, at Jay, and then at the rest of the family. She smiled and said, "Good, I thought you were going to tell me that I had AIDS." She started laughing, and everyone followed suit and laughed and laughed. Everyone dreaded to see her response as she was told the horrible news. The way she handled the situation, however, confirmed what they already knew: Autumn was a fighter.

Since Autumn's fever had broken, and she had gained strength, the doctor said that they were going to bring the baby in and let her hold her for the first time. What a wonderful moment it was when Autumn got to hold her precious baby girl in her arms. Since Kaley was a few weeks premature, she looked so tiny in her preemie outfit. Again, so many photos were being taken that baby Kaley must have been seeing stars in her eyes from the flashes of light. The next few days were touch-and-go for Autumn, and they would only allow the baby to stay in the room as long as the mother's fever was down.

The oncologist did a test to see if the disease was in the bone marrow, and in fact, it was. They told the family that Autumn had less than a four percent chance of making it, but since she was young, that was in her favor. However, the surgery and the loss of so much blood had weakened her body and made her less able to fight the disease. The oncologist came to speak with Jay and Autumn about the results and treatments; no one else was allowed in the room.

Cathy stated that she remembered thinking, "four percent chance!" It just did not register. She said that she was so angry because the oncologist would not allow them to be with their daughter when he broke the news to her that she had very little chance of surviving the disease. Then, it hit her, "four percent!" It was at that moment this grief-stricken mother realized that if her daughter did not get a miracle, she would die.

Eddie and Cathy were glad that Jay was in there with Autumn, holding her hand as the doctor spoke to her. The rest of the family could only watch them through the glass window as they received the news; they were both so brave and strong. The parents' hearts were broken as they watched their daughter go through the most difficult time in her life. They felt so helpless.

One day as Cathy was standing by Autumn's bed and her daughter was feeding Kaley, she said, "Mom, I am scared; I do not know if I can be a good mother?" Cathy assured her daughter that she would be just fine.

The next evening, on June 8, it was just Autumn and her mother in the room. Cathy stood at the foot of her daughter's bed and rubbed her swollen feet as she gave her cheerleader speech: "Autumn, we are going to beat this disease, and after we beat it, we are going to go on the Oprah show and tell your story and testify to the fact that God is a God of miracles." She went on to say that she could see at least fifteen angels standing around her bed.

Autumn looked at her mother and said so seriously, "More!" She always had to get in the last word. Mother and Daughter just looked at each other and smiled.

Tommy and Cheryl, two very dear friends of the family, had taken Kaley home with them from the hospital and were taking care of her so that Jay, Cathy, and Eddie could stay with Autumn. They would bring the baby back to the hospital each day so that Autumn could spend some time with her.

There were literally twenty to thirty people at the hospital at any given time to show support to Autumn and the family. Church family, co-workers, and friends were always coming by the hospital, leaving cards, and offering encouraging words and prayers. They could not always come in and see Autumn, but since she was in a room that had windows, they could see her and wave at her. Everyone was praying and believing that God was going to heal her.

Every day the nurses checked Autumn's blood count to see if they could start the chemo. They were having difficulty drawing blood, and Autumn looked like a pincushion with so many punctures and bruises.

It was June 9. Autumn said, "Mom I don't understand why I have to go through all this, but if by me going through this, I can make a difference in someone's life, then it will be worth it." It was such courage and strong words of faith coming from someone so sick. Hearing her speak those words gave the rest of the family strength to endure when it seemed their whole world was crumbling around them.

There were many nurses in and out of Autumn's room, but there was one in particular that Autumn had talked to quite often during the past four days. The nurse came into the room and said, "Autumn, my shift is over, and I will be going home soon and will not be back until next week, but I wanted to come in and tell you that if I do not see you again, just having the privilege to know you these past few days has impacted my life forever. Thank you!"

Autumn looked at her mother and smiled, and Cathy smiled back at her. Her mom knew at that moment that her daughter was thinking about the conversation the two of them had had earlier about making a difference in even one person's life. She felt that what she was going through was worth it, if nothing more than for this one woman's life to have been touched. What a testimony of faith!

Autumn's parents had been at the hospital pretty much around the clock, and since their daughter was doing so well, the couple decided to go home for a few hours to shower and try to get some rest. Furthermore, Autumn had insisted on that night being Ma Maw's night to spend with her. Ma Maw was Autumn's grandmother, Jan McGuffey, whom she loved dearly.

Eddie went on to work the next morning, and Cathy went back to the hospital. She arrived about 5:30 a.m. Jan said that Autumn had gotten up at 5:00 a.m. and went to the bathroom. She complained that her head was hurting, so she lay back down and went to sleep. Jan said that her granddaughter had gone through a very rough night, but had finally fallen into a restful sleep. Jan then left to go home to shower. Cathy didn't want to awaken Autumn; she was sleeping so well.

Jay was there also when the oncologist came in. He did not wake Autumn either and said that since her blood count was good, they would finally be able to start the chemotherapy later that day. Words could not express the joy and relief that family felt at hearing those words.

At about 9:30 a.m., Jay left to go to work. Then about thirty minutes or so after the doctor left, Autumn began making a strange sound as she struggled to breathe. Cathy felt that something was wrong, so she went and asked a nurse if she would help move Autumn up in the bed because she didn't seem to be breathing right and was making a gurgling sound. The nurse took her vital signs and asked Cathy if Autumn had sleep apnea, and she said, "No." The nurse said the reason she was asking was that Autumn's breathing would stop for few seconds, which was abnormal.

The nurse rushed out to get the doctor, and Autumn's mom quickly called her husband and Jay to tell them what was happening. She tried to wake up her daughter by saying, "Autumn, Kaley will be here shortly to see you; wake up." As her mother touched her daughter's cheek, it seemed that she would try to open her eyes, but couldn't.

The frantic mother tried to keep her voice calm as she spoke to her daughter. Then Autumn's left arm started restricting, and for the first time, she saw a tear roll down her daughter's cheek. When the doctor and nurses came in, he told Autumn's mom to keep talking to her. He said, "There is a chance that she might hear you." Cathy began to quote her daughter's favorite scripture, Psalm 23, in hopes that she could hear her.

Eddie and Jay had arrived at this point, and Eddie was helping them get the bed out of the room and down to ICU, so they could give her the care she needed. A nurse told the family where to wait.

Eddie had barely entered the waiting room when an announcement came over the speaker saying, "Code Blue." The number that was announced was Autumn's room number. Cathy said that she felt like her heart was going to explode in her chest.

The oncologist eventually appeared and told the family that they had gotten Autumn back, and that she was on life support. They were making plans to fly her to the Vanderbilt University Hospital in Nashville, Tennessee. Autumn had bleeding on her brain and the hospital in Bowling Green had done all that they could for her.

The parents were not allowed to ride down to Vanderbilt University in the helicopter, so they travelled by car. While they were in route, they called everyone they could think of and asked them to pray. Pray! Pray! The pastor, his wife, and many family and friends went with them and stayed the night.

The concerned family and friends slept very little that night as they sat in the waiting room anxiously awaiting some news about Autumn's condition. The bleeding on her brain had caused it to swell, and the doctors were testing to see if there was any brain activity.

When the doctor met with the family that day, June 11th, he told them that Autumn was brain-dead, and there was nothing else they could do for her. He also informed them that the law required tests be done to make sure that there were no brain waves. The test showed no brain activity, and she was taken off life support.

Autumn's mom said that at that moment she felt like she was living someone else's life, and that she was in a bad nightmare and just wanted to wake up. Within two weeks she had lost her mother and her daughter.

She questioned, "How could this be happening to us; Why God? Autumn was just twenty-two years old; she was so full of life. Each day she lived it to the fullest capacity, and she loved you, Lord. Why?" The family felt that their hearts were shattered and their faith was severely shaken. Jay and his parents, John and Pat, were also devastated; their precious grandbaby was now left without her mother.

The drive home from Vanderbilt that day was the longest drive ever. Eddie and Cathy had held on to the hope that the Lord was going to heal their daughter, but while it was not God's plan to heal her in this life, He did ultimately give her a complete healing—everlasting. Cathy was deeply saddened at the thought of not being able to say good-bye to her daughter. She felt like there were so many unsaid things that she had wanted to say to her little girl.

That evening, when the McGuffey family arrived back home, their son and his wife were with them. Steven came in and checked his email and said, "Mom and dad, come here quick!" He had opened an email and didn't know who had sent it. It spelled FAMILY and each letter stood for a word.

The email read:

F–ather

A–nd

M–other

I–

L–ove

Y–ou

The whole family started to weep; it was as if Autumn were speaking right to their hearts.

Their son Steven, along with some friends, went back to Autumn's home to get the dress that she was to wear at her funeral, along with the jewelry. There was no doubt in Cathy's mind that Autumn was to wear that lavender gown from Dillard's that she had said made her feel so beautiful. Little did this mother know that at the time she was buying the dress that her daughter would be wearing it at her funeral.

When Steven came in with the jewelry, and it was taken out of the box, a note fell on the floor. Autumn's mom picked it up, and it read: "The necklace is for my daughter; this was given to me by my father." Autumn had written the note two years before. There was no way to know that she would later have a girl, but God knew. Subsequently, the family would find several other notes, along with her jewelry, that were meant for her daughter to have.

The next two days at the funeral home were filled with so many different emotions. Literally hundreds of people came through during the visitation to offer their condolences. The family was deeply touched. The McGuffey's had no idea of how many lives their daughter had impacted.

On the day of the funeral, all the seats were filled to capacity; many people had to stand during the service. Cathy thought about her dream that she had shared with Autumn only a week before about a funeral home filled with hundreds of people. At the time of the dream, she thought it was her son's funeral that she was being shown, but in reality, it was her daughter's funeral.

Previously, Autumn had recorded a song called "Midnight Cry" on a cassette tape for Cathy's brother-in-law to listen to. She was singing the song "a cappella." The song was played at Autumn's funeral. Her voice was so crisp and clear; it was as if she were there in person singing the song. Cathy said that she remembered thinking: "My darling Autumn, you may be with the Lord, but you are still ministering to our hearts."

Eddie shared some very emotional words at his daughter's funeral. She would have been very proud of him.

The family was greatly comforted by the cards and letters they received in the days that followed. These words of love and show of support were such an encouragement to Jay and the rest of our family. They were very thankful for the prayers that went forth on their behalf, because at the time, it was difficult for them to find the words or strength to pray themselves.

After Autumn's death, Jay sold their home in Tennessee; he was never able to live there anymore. Jay and Kaley moved in with Autumn's parents, and they helped care for Kaley. About a year later, Jay's parents, John and Pat Redmond, moved back to town, and Jay and Kaley moved in with them for a while. They all shared in helping to raise little Kaley.

Every time Cathy held Kaley, she could not help but think about her daughter. As the months went by, they were amazed at how much Kaley was starting to look like her mother. The McGuffey's were very blessed and thankful that God had given Jay this beautiful little girl and had given them their first grandchild to love. A part of their daughter would live on through Kaley.

Over the next several days Cathy had many questions that she would ask God: "Lord why? Why? Why? Why didn't You take me instead of my daughter? She was so young; she loved You. She was a great witness for You and was making a difference in so many lives. Autumn had so much living yet to do."

Through all of Cathy's questioning, God was silent. When someone asks us a question, we feel obligated to give them some kind of answer. But God often speaks to us in silence. It is in those silent moments that you prove your trust in God. Cathy stated, "I thought that I had a strong relationship with Christ before losing my mom and daughter, but through their deaths, I came to realize that there is so much more to God's love and understanding that I had never known."

During this time Autumn's mom said that she prayed: "Lord, You said in your Word that You are faithful and will not let us to be tempted beyond what we can bear. Lord, I think that we are at that point right now. We cannot handle any more, Lord." She cried out day and night.

The pain was so great. This grieving mother stated that she opened her Bible and started reading in the Book of Job, and her thoughts were: "Oh God, how could Job bear the pain of losing all of his children?" She remembered reading the poem, "Footprints in the Sand," and for once in her life, she truly understood what it meant. The Lord would surely have to carry them through the next several months—and years, because they could not bear the pain alone.

Cathy began to look at Autumn's journals and could not believe what she was reading. She had written specific details concerning her funeral: the color of the casket, the kind of flowers, and the songs to be sung. She sat there crying and thanking God. Though they didn't know what their daughter's requests were at the time of her funeral, they had fulfilled almost every one of them. It had to have been divine intervention from God.

After Autumn's death the family received a call from National City Bank asking them to attend a special luncheon where they were going to honor their daughter. Autumn had previously worked at the bank. When Jay, Eddie, and Cathy arrived, they found it to be a very special event. To their surprise, Dr. Gary A. Ransdell, President of Western Kentucky University was there and presented them with their daughter's diploma. It was a very emotional moment for all of them. The family was honored, and accepted their daughter's diploma with pride.

Autumn's dreams and desires were then complete: She had married a Christian man, had a home of their own, had experienced the joy of being a mother (though for a brief time), and had graduated from WKU with a degree in Home Health Administration.

Days were filled with memories, questions, tears, and frustrations. Autumn's mom recalled a song she had heard after the death of Autumn that brought her great comfort and peace; it was "Through the Fire." All she could do was weep as she listened. The song seemed to put it all into perspective.

"So many times I've questioned certain
circumstances, things I
could not understand.
Many times in trials, weakness blurs my vision then my
frustration gets so out of hand.
It's then I am reminded I've never been forsaken I've never had
to stand the test alone.
As I look at all the victories the spirit rises up in me and it's
through the fire my weakness is made strong."

Cathy stated that she vividly remembers a phone call that they received one night.

She had discussed with her husband, Eddie, that she would like to attend the "Crabb Fest" which was being held about eighty miles from where they lived in Bowling Green, Kentucky. The Crabb Family music had always ministered to them, and at that time this couple needed all the strength they could get. She figured it was probably too late to get tickets since it was only a few days until the event.

(Crabb Fest was a Christian music event hosted by The Crabb Family. It lasted about four days and featured many of the top Southern Gospel groups. The event was held each year in Owensboro, Kentucky.)

One night the phone rang, and it was Cathy and Eddie's friend Carson, who worked with the Crabb Family. He said that if they wanted to attend the "Crabb Fest," Gerald Crabb would have tickets at the ticket booth with their names on them for each night.

Cathy thanked him and hung up the phone and turned to her husband with tears running down her cheeks and told him, "You are not going to believe it," and she gave him the news. Nobody but God knew that she and her husband had just discussed wanting to attend the concert. They cried together. God was letting them know that He had not left them nor forsaken them, but was hearing their prayers.

When the day finally came, and Cathy and Eddie arrived at the Crabb Fest, their tickets were at the ticket booth as promised. This couple, which had suffered such a loss, felt so empty inside and needed desperately to be ministered to that night. And that was exactly what happened. During the concert, I brought Eddie, Cathy, and their granddaughter Kaley up on the stage to stand beside the Crabb Family, and I shared with the audience about the loss of their daughter, Autumn. Then I talked about how blessed this family was to still have part of their daughter with them, referring to Kaley.

As they stood with us on the stage, I felt it was appropriate to dedicate a special song to them; we sang "Through the Fire." The whole atmosphere was filled with the presence of the Lord. There were about five thousand people present and just about the whole audience were on their feet weeping and praising God. Cathy said that as she stood there listening to the lyrics of that God-given song, she felt such peace. She further stated, "It was at that time that we knew we were going to make it through."

Cathy and Eddie both stated that they could now say from the depths of their hearts that it is better to have loved and lost, than to have never loved at all. Their lives have been enriched by the beautiful gifts the Lord gave to them when he gave them their children and grandchildren.

Their son, Steven, and his wife, Karen, now have two children, Emma and Andrew.

Jay has married a wonderful Christian woman, Dena. Kaley is now blessed with a mom who loves her very much, and a baby sister, Kendra.

A few summers ago Kaley attended Youth Camp at the Church of God campgrounds in Lexington, Kentucky. It was the same camp where the McGuffey's daughter and son had attended many years earlier.

Something wonderful happened during the youth camp, and Kaley's grandfather Eddie and her new mom, Dena, were there to witness it. Kaley accepted Christ into her heart as her personal Savior! Seconds later, Cathy received two text messages simultaneously from Eddie and Dena telling her about Kaley's conversion. She sat at work and cried, thanking her heavenly Father for allowing Eddie to be a part of his granddaughter's greatest moment in life. Surely the angels in heaven rejoiced together on that special day.

God has opened many other doors for Eddie and Cathy McGuffey since the death of their daughter. Eddie is a minister and Cathy is involved in a ministry called, "Princess of the King." Cathy speaks at conferences and ladies' retreats. If you are interested in Cathy speaking at a meeting you may contact her at www.clmminstries.com.

This great family has gone through the fire.

They made their journey with many unanswered questions, yet their faith in God was strong enough to carry them through; they never looked back and never lost trust.

Through the fire their weakness was made strong. To God be the glory!

An entry from Autumn's journal date 5-3-98

Now another day draws to an end. I thank you Lord, for what has been.

If I have mistaken or sinned, I pray tonight, that my sins you forgive.

Life is precious, and full of gold. We should learn to take it slow.

For one day, we will leave this world, and if prepared, we will live with you eternal.

Until that time, just be with me. Keep me safe and continue to love me.

Help me to learn from all my mistakes, and teach others to learn the same way.

Use me Lord and prepare me, so I may lead someone to your kingdom.

Sometimes we all fall, but Lord You are the greatest Friend of all.

You pick us up and lead us straight, so that one day Lord, we may meet at the pearly gates.

Loved ones and friends that have gone on to be with You, soon we will see in a new view.

Just keep me in your way divine. Help me Lord to let my light shine. I love You Lord, and just want to say, Thank You Lord, for another day.

Amen,
Autumn

Chapter 3

Victories without Fighting

A preacher once said that Satan sets traps and stumbling blocks early in our lives to try to confuse or misdirect us from finding our destiny. I'm sure that this statement could raise a lot of debate among the great theologians and Bible scholars of our day. However, that is how Rebecca feels about the path of life she has traveled. After reading her story, I think you will understand why she might entertain those feelings.

Rebecca grew up in Michigan. She has one sibling, a brother who is a year older. As young children growing up, they were a very close family. Her dad worked for one of the auto industries in the area. Mom stayed at home where she kept the house, cooked, and took care of the children.

The family had lots of friends and was very involved in the church that they attended. They hardly ever missed a church service. In fact, going on Sunday night, Sunday morning, and Wednesday night was not an option; attendance was mandatory for their family. Their church often held revival meetings that could last for several days. They were always there fulfilling their obligation to God and to the church.

Their Christian faith was a vital part of their lives. Rebecca's mom would gather the family each night and have devotions, even if they had a guest in their home. Rebecca said that many nights she sat through the mandatory devotions, but with much resentment. Yet looking back, she realized that those times were precious memories being etched in her memory bank.

Dad was a hard-working father, but it was Mom that brought the strong sense of security to the family. Each played their role: Mom was the rule maker and Dad was the stern enforcer.

They appeared to be the perfect Christian family, yet the foundation of this family was shaken by a divorce. Rebecca and her brother were traumatized. They were just fourteen and fifteen years old when they were given the heartbreaking news that their parents were getting a divorce.

They soon learned that divorce changes everything. The traditional two-parent lifestyle that they were accustomed to had now changed to living with a single parent—Mom. Even though Mom continued to be the same God-fearing woman, it was difficult for her to step into the role of disciplinarian.

Things changed as the two teenagers began to explore what they thought were greener pastures. Up to this point, their whole world had revolved around church and family. However, the trauma of divorce and natural curiosity led them into doing things they should not have done. They were too young to realize at the time that the choices they were making would affect the rest of their lives.

Rebecca was a popular high-school cheerleader and very involved in academics. As fate would have it, she met a boy with a very bad reputation. Though others tried to warn her, there was something about the "bad boy" image that appealed to her. She fell really hard for this guy. During this same time she had also been introduced to the world of drugs and alcohol. Such things had never been tolerated in the Christian home where she had been raised, so I would say that this "forbidden fruit" probably looked especially appealing to her.

By the time Rebecca was fifteen years old, she was pregnant with her boyfriend's child. She was just sixteen when her baby was born. Two years later the couple were married.

After just about three weeks into the marriage, Rebecca began to see a side of her husband that she hadn't seen before. She always knew that he was quick tempered, but up this to point, he had never physically harmed her. Things quickly changed, however, and the abuse that would last for several years began.

The beatings were so severe at times that she would be knocked unconscious. One night, while her husband was in a fit of rage, she fled to a neighbor's home to seek refuge. The beating had been so horrible that most of her clothes had been torn from her body.

The physical abuse took place at least once a month. After each beating, he would offer lame apologies and utter false regrets, and each time he would win her sympathy. She knew that she was holding onto a false sense of hope, but she wanted to believe that for the sake of their child he would change. Deep down, however, she knew it was just a matter of time until something would trigger the next mad rage, and another beating.

Weekends were especially a dread. He and some of his buddies would go off on a drinking binge that would last for several days. When he finally decided to come home, he was ready for a fight. The smallest thing would set him off, and once again she would be the target of his fury.

After six years into the abusive marriage, Rebecca gave birth to another son. Not long after this, her husband began to show favoritism toward the younger son. At the same time, he began to display abusive behavior toward the older son. He was extremely rough on the older son and critical of everything he did.

After returning home from work one evening, she found her eight-year-old screaming, and noticed that he had a bleeding cut on his forehead. After inquiring into what had happened, she found out that his dad had hit him because he had not made up the bed. At that point, she knew that she and her children must leave. She had suffered about ten years in an abusive relationship and probably would have continued to endure the abuse if her husband hadn't started abusing her son. She knew that she must take any steps necessary to get her children out of that hostile environment.

Rebecca began to devise a plan to leave that would not create suspicion. She convinced her husband to go to the grocery store to pick up a list of things she needed. While he was away, she hurriedly threw a few clothes together, and she and the children left.

The next several months were very emotional. Her husband repeatedly threatened her, and she lived in constant fear. She became a nervous wreck. Though she had moved in with her mother, she still lived in fear. Many nights she would barricade the door out of fear that he might come in the middle of the night in a fit of rage, break in, and harm her and the children. Another fear that tormented her was that she would encounter him on her way to or from work.

Rebecca had lived in a prison of abuse for many years in which no one, not even her closest friends, knew what she was going through. She felt she couldn't let anyone know what was really going on in her secret world of hell.

According to statistics of battered women, 3.9 million women are physically abused by their partners daily, which means that every nine seconds a woman is physically abused by her husband. Ninety-five percent of assaults on spouses or ex-spouses are committed by men against women. (See www.asafeplaceforhelp.org.) http://www.asafeplaceforhelp.org/ Furthermore, most people experiencing relationship violence do not tell others what goes on at home.

When this is the case, these individuals' lives become a living nightmare. For Rebecca, living this secret life of abuse and torment seemed to be the norm. She had kept her abuse a secret from her family and her closest friends.

Not only had she covered up the secret life of physical abuse inflicted upon her by her ex-husband for ten years, but also she was dealing with other painful memories. A family member had raped her at the age of four. The sexual molestation lasted for eight years, until she reached the age of twelve.

She doesn't remember the abuser ever threatening her if she didn't keep silent. She just felt that she could never tell anyone. No one had any suspicion that this abuse was taking place. As a result of this horrible experience as a child, Rebecca always felt dirty. She was robbed of her innocence at such an early age. When little girls should be playing with dolls and toys, she was living in a nightmare of sexual abuse.

Rebecca and the boys had moved in with her mother for a couple of months. Though she still dealt with the fear of her husband, it was helpful to be in a Christian home as she struggled to find some answers and some badly needed serenity. Since her mom was a godly woman who relied heavily on the Bible and prayer for strength and guidance, it was definitely the atmosphere and influence that she needed.

She and the boys soon found their own place to live in the town where she grew up. It was near her mother and about two hours away from her abusive husband.

It took about one year for her to get enough courage to file for a divorce. Then it took several months before the divorce became final. The wait was nerve-wracking! She hoped and prayed for the day that there would be some peace and normalcy in the lives of her and the children.

Over time, things had gotten much better between Rebecca and the children's father. Since he had met another lady, his attention was focused elsewhere. The hostile phone calls and harassment eventually stopped. Not long after the couple met, they married. For Rebecca, it was like a ray of sunshine after a very long storm.

With the help and support of family and friends, Rebecca was able to go back to school and begin to focus on raising her two boys whom she loved very much. She enrolled in a Christian college and earned a Bachelor of Arts degree. She began indulging in Bible studies and prayer groups, earnestly seeking to find some stability in her life.

Yet, even with all the activity in her life, she still found herself struggling with a deep depression. It felt like these thoughts of depression were sucking her down into a bed of quicksand.

What a blessing it was when Rebecca became acquainted with a wonderful Christian counselor. The lady counselor seemed to have a lot of wisdom and God-given discernment. She quickly recognized that something in Rebecca's past was haunting her, and she was determined to search it out. One day she asked, "Were you ever molested as a child?"

Rebecca was in shock because of the question. She knew that she had never told anyone of the horrible abuse that had started almost twenty-five years earlier. She began to open up and share everything with her counselor. It was very painful to relive the horrible memories and to talk about those things that had haunted her for so long. On the other hand, she felt a sense of relief as she began to open up, and the heavy load began to lift.

Afterward she shared with her mother and father what had happened to her as a child. They were shocked. As she began to unlock the secret chambers of her past, others in the family felt that they could come forward and share their horrible experiences as well. The same man had molested her brother, along with other children in the neighborhood.

One Sunday, in her home church, she went forward and asked her pastor to pray for her because she was fighting a deep depression. He found that hard to believe, because she had done such a good job hiding her true feelings. That night as they began to pray and trust God for total deliverance, Rebecca felt that the chains of depression were broken.

Looking back, she now feels as if Satan had set a trap for her. All of the abuse, both sexual and physical, and all of the dark secrets had baited the trap of depression, and she had been caught in it for many years. Now at last she began to experience the feeling of freedom. She was overjoyed, and anxious to share the liberating gospel of Jesus Christ to all who would listen. She began speaking at a lot of Christian singles groups.

For nine years Rebecca filled the role of a single mother. She worked to provide for her and her two children. After work, her evenings were filled with assisting the children with homework, school projects, ballgames, and church activities. Also during that time, she had gone back to school to further her education. There were many long nights of studying. After very little sleep, she would drag herself out of bed and go to work from nine to five.

That was a very difficult time, yet her determination and faith in God helped provide the strength she needed to see it through. She did everything within her power to provide a good life for her two sons. Keeping a strong relationship with God was very important through the years of single parenting. It also helped her to deal with the bitterness, the pain, and the haunting memories of the past.

The father of her children, now remarried, had made a total change in his life. He was very sorry for the pain he had put them through. He often asked her for forgiveness. Since Rebecca had such a strong relationship with God, she found it in her heart to forgive her ex-husband. Life was now better than it had been for many years, and things were somewhat normal. No abuse. No drama. No secrets.

It was evident that God had placed the right people in her life to help her get through. Those were the healing years!

When Rebecca started conducting Bible studies for singles, she found it was something she relished. Preparing the lessons required much prayer and study. Therefore, it brought about spiritual growth in her life. Life for Rebecca was good, and it seemed to be getting better each day.

One night in December 1990 Rebecca met another single parent. He approached her and began asking questions about her lesson regarding parenting. She talked about the importance of praying for your children and asking the Lord to guard them by placing His angels around them.

She shared with him the story of how her two boys had been in a terrible accident while traveling to see their father. It was the first time her sixteen-year-old son had driven to his father's. She didn't understand why, but she had a terrible feeling before they left. Because of this feeling, she prayed for the boys and asked God to put angels under, over, and all around the car.

Fifteen minutes after leaving home, her son lost control of the car. It crossed over to the other side of the highway, almost hitting a school bus head-on. Instead of hitting the bus, the car hit the median and went airborne at sixty-five miles an hour. The car then rolled three times and was completely crushed, except for two little spots where the boys were seated. The car was totaled, but the boys were miraculously spared.

Her seven-year-old son had a broken arm and was running down the highway in shock. The bus driver ran after him. All the while the child was running, he was yelling, "I have to get to my mom."

She continued to share with the gentleman how she believed that God had protected her boys as He gave His angels charge over them. The oldest son had stated that he felt the weight of something sitting over him and holding him in his seat.

Rebecca had no idea at that time that she was talking to the man that would be her husband in a few months. He had been through a very painful divorce. His ex-wife was a severe drug addict. He had been given custody of his three children. Therefore, her lesson on Christian parenting and interceding for your children seemed to really hit home for him.

After the Bible study, several of those attending went out for ice cream in order to become more acquainted with one another. The man was still very broken from his divorce and seemed to draw strength from Rebecca. It had been several years since she had weathered a similar storm, and by this time she had become settled.

It wasn't long before they began to realize that they had an attraction for one another, and he asked her out for a date. She thought that he was attractive—six foot seven, with dark hair, and very funny at times. On their third date he asked if she would marry him. Though she thought it was a bit fast, one year later they got married.

Suddenly there were two families blended into one. It was good to have a man around the house, a companion to enjoy the blessings of life with, and someone to share the not-so-good things with. Yet, it was very different.

All of them had to make quite a few adjustments. Her oldest son at that time was going to college and spent very little time at home. The ten-year-old missed his big brother a lot, especially since he had to share his mother and his life with four people he barely knew. It was very difficult, but they pulled together and made it work. Though there were many hurdles to overcome, Rebecca and her husband stayed true to God and to each other. Both parents worked very hard to provide a good home for their family.

About twelve years into the marriage, they faced a new challenge. They became temporary foster parents of two little girls who had been taken from their home due to their mother's drug abuse. After one year the girls were put back into their home with the mother, who appeared to be clean from drugs. After six weeks she overdosed on drugs and the children were permanently taken from her. Rebecca and her husband had the option to adopt. It was an easy decision since they had already bonded with the girls and loved them very much.

In 2004 the couple adopted the two beautiful little girls. It was a bittersweet situation: It was sad that the children had been taken away from their mother, yet it was such joy knowing that those precious little girls had a safe home and loving and caring parents. At that time all their children were gone from home, so having the little ones around was like a breath of fresh air.

After the adoption their lives changed dramatically. Instead of just sitting around the house, their afternoons were filled with fun and laughter as the couple watched the girls playing with dolls and toys. They also enjoyed taking the girls on shopping trips, looking for little girl things. Christmas, Easter, and birthdays were especially fun; life was great and exciting.

Rebecca worked in banking, which was greatly affected during the banking crisis. Her branch of operations was sold, and she was left without a job. For quite a while she and her husband had discussed the idea of moving to Arkansas to her husband's hometown. Since he was retired and she was out of work, it seemed like the right time to move. The move would be especially great for her husband; he would be so happy to live near his family again. The move was finally completed, and one of the first things they did was to find a good church to attend.

Within a short time, however, a dark cloud moved in and settled over them. In the spring of 2005 her husband's brother unexpectedly died at the age of forty. Her husband was devastated. Eight months later, her husband's youngest son died of an overdose at the age of twenty-five. He had been mixing drugs and alcohol. He had gotten the drugs from his mother, the ex-wife of Rebecca's husband. The pain of losing a child is a horrible experience, especially under those circumstances. Eight months later, the ex-wife died of a drug overdose. Four months later, the sister of Rebecca's husband died. Eight months after that, his mother passed away. And then, six months after his mother's death, he lost his father. Thus, in a period of thirty-four months, there were six deaths in the family. He was devastated, to say the least.

Having to deal with so many family deaths was almost more than Rebecca's husband could handle. In fact, he almost lost his mind. During this time he had been put on medication to calm his nerves, yet the pills could not soothe the aching he had in his heart. He became an emotional wreck.

Rebecca felt that she had to be the strong one in the family. They had adopted two little girls that needed a lot of care and attention. Plus, her husband needed her to be his wife and best friend, someone strong to lean on and to offer him comfort.

Those years were definitely trying times, and she found herself falling apart inside. Trying to hold down her new job that involved much travel, while being a homemaker and giving the girls and her husband the care and support they needed, was just about more than she could bear. She felt guilty to be falling apart emotionally when everyone else needed her so badly. Her emotions were like a crack in a dam—little by little the leaks get bigger and bigger until eventually the dam breaks with an uncontrollable force. She felt that at any moment she was going to explode.

One day as Rebecca was suffering from a stress-related headache, she ran across a bottle of pain pills. It was an old bottle of pills that she had kept from a surgery she had undergone several months earlier. She took one of the pills, and in a short time the headache was gone, along with all the emotional pressure. She could function as a new burst of energy flowed through her body. At that time all she could think about was what a blessing it was to find some relief.

In a couple of days she took another pill, and just like the other, it seemed to make her strong again and enable her to be what her family needed. It wasn't long until she was taking one pill each day just to get the feeling, the energy, and the escape from reality.

No one knew, except her, about her newfound crutch. Everything seemed great for a while. She saw nothing wrong with taking a pill a day; yet it wasn't long until one pill wasn't enough. As the pills began to lose their effectiveness, she began to double up on them. She would occasionally go to her physician to obtain a prescription for pain medication—treatment for migraine headaches.

By the time the second year rolled around, the drugs were defiantly in control. The feeling of depression became very frequent, which only called for more drugs.

Within the second year Rebecca was taking fifteen to twenty pain pills per day. On most days it was twenty pills of Tramadol at fifty milligrams each. Three-hundred milligrams a day can be lethal; she was taking one thousand milligrams a day. She began to suffer severely from migraine headaches, probably caused by the excessive drug use. Nevertheless, she used her headaches as an excuse to get more pain medication. At that time she was seeing two doctors to get enough drugs to supply her addiction. It wasn't long until she was getting drugs online also. She thus had found three different sources for drugs.

The drugs were, without doubt, the controlling force in her life. She was always afraid that she would run out of pills and would not be able to get what she needed. She had become insensitive to everybody and everything around her. The only thing that mattered was the drugs. She lived in constant fear that she would die by an overdose or that God would just take her out. The woman that once loved God with all her heart, loved studying the word, and going to church had changed into an addict who lived for the next fix. She began looking for reasons not to attend church, and the Bible was seldom touched. Her drugs had become her god.

All this time no one knew what was going on in Rebecca's life. She still held down her job, did a few things around the house, and went to church occasionally, while being under the influence of drugs. Once again she found herself caught in a trap of secrecy. (This is how Satan does his work.) In a time of desperation she had turned to something that seemed to be innocent—something just to help her cope with the pressures of life. Two years later, she was caught in his trap.

Within the second year things began to change drastically, due to the excessive drug abuse. The person who was once so vibrant and happy now lived in a state of depression. She became very reclusive and withdrawn from the world, even those she loved. She felt that she had nothing to give anyone. It was a struggle just to get through the day. She often thought that death would be the only way out of the prison that she was in. What had started out as a good feeling had ended up a living nightmare.

Everything around her was falling apart. The mail would lie for days without being opened; bills would go unpaid. She felt that she couldn't stand the pressure of reading what was in the envelopes. The calls to her children, parents, and friends became less and less frequent. They had all become very concerned about her emotional state, yet they thought she was just struggling with the deaths that had occurred in the family. They were not aware of the drugs, and she was too ashamed to tell them.

Rebecca's life was spinning out of control. Her work required a great deal of travel, and she would schedule trips out of town just to get away from everyone. She was headed for complete destruction. She knew it, but couldn't seem to do anything about it. Her every move was planned around the drugs; they were in total control. She was not only dealing with this evil influence, but was also dealing with a feeling of shame. It was as though there was a spirit that accompanied the drugs.

She would often hurt people by her words and actions. Hiding behind the role of the housewife, the businesswoman, and the Christian was starting to become impossible. The facade was wearing thin. She felt like there was a huge wall surrounding her that was about to crumble, and she was going to be crushed beneath the rubble.

It seemed at times that life had dealt her more than her share of pain. First, it was the eight years of sexual abuse as a child by a family member that had robbed her of her innocence. Then came the twelve years of physical abuse that became almost unbearable at times. Now she was suffering from the drug abuse that was destroying her life.

She had gone through the fire over and over again, yet God had delivered her every time. Once again she needed His help. Rebecca loved God, her husband, her children, and her family, but everything had become a blur and distorted. She knew she was getting to the point that something had to happen; yet, she could tell no one. At times she begged God to take the addiction from her, but she never seemed to get an answer.

One day while channel surfing on the TV, she heard a line in a song, "He never promised victories without fighting." Rebecca remembered what she had learned from Bible study: The word of God teaches us that sometimes we have to fight to gain victory; God will not always do it for you, but He will do it with you. Those words brought hope to a very desperate situation.

Rebecca felt great joy as she flushed her drugs down the toilet. As they went down the drain, she said, "I can do this." She fell on her knees and began to call on God, asking Him for deliverance. This time it was different. She was ready to do her part; she was ready to fight.

Rebecca later found out that she was watching a Bill Gaither program featuring *The Best of The Crabb Family*. The song she was listening to was "Through the Fire." What a ray of hope she had discovered in that one line of a song. Shortly after hearing the song, Rebecca went on the

Internet and downloaded the song. Each time she began to experience a feeling of withdrawal, she turned the song up to high volume and claimed her victory. She listened to it over and over.

Looking back, she now sees how her drug addiction fueled other addictions, but she had reached the place where she was now ready to lay them all down, and she did. Even her seven-year-old daughter could see a drastic change in her mom. It wasn't long until both daughters knew every word of the song "Through the Fire." They had heard the words so many times that they couldn't help but memorize them.

Rebecca didn't go through the same severity of drug withdrawals that most recovering drug addicts have to contend with, even though she quit cold turkey. She attributes her success to Jesus Christ and the powerful words in the song that they had listened to so many times: "He never promised victories without fighting."

Six months after flushing the drugs she had to go and help her mother who was battling cancer. Since her mother was on strong pain medication, Rebecca had access to all sorts of pills, yet she wasn't even tempted. Praise God! He will take you through the fire again and again.

As of 2010, Rebecca had shared her story with me by phone and email, and I had seen pictures of her and her family, but I had never personally met her. One Sunday morning in June 2010, I was the guest speaker at a church in central Arkansas. As I got up to speak, a lady and two young ladies came in and sat down in the congregation. I noticed that it was Rebecca. I was very happy to see them there. At the end of the message, as I gave the invitation, one of the two young ladies, along with her mother, Rebecca, came to the altar. That morning I had the privilege of praying the sinner's prayer with that precious young lady.

Today, Rebecca is spending quality time with her family and enjoying the new commitment that she has made with her Lord and Savior Jesus Christ.

Chapter 4

Things I Could Not Understand

I met Bob Bain in the late 1970s; he was on the music committee at the Church of God camp meetings in Lexington, Kentucky. He was a very upbeat guy and extremely sincere about his walk with God.

Just by watching him from the audience you could tell that he loved what he was doing as he led the choir and the congregation in praise and worship. What I didn't know then was that he continually struggled with the dreaded disease of diabetes, which took him from one trial to another.

Throughout the next ten years we failed to keep in touch with each other. I didn't see Bob again until the late 1990s. At that time my family and I were traveling across the country doing concerts. One night while in Alabama Bob showed up at one of those events. We talked for quite a while, trying to catch up on everything. He shared with me some of the setbacks that he had dealt with through the years, and it was very obvious that the disease had taken its toll on my ol' friend. Yet, he wasn't bitter or angry with God. He was just glad to be alive and glad to be at the concert.

After that meeting we continued to do about three concerts a year in the Northeast Alabama area, and on most occasions Bob would be there. Each time I saw my friend, I could see how much more his health had declined; yet he never complained. On the contrary, he appeared to be the happiest person in the audience. Throughout the concert he would clap his hands or sing along with us, and occasionally, I would hear him yell out an "Amen" or "Praise the Lord."

His trials made my problems seem very minimal. Yet I'm sure that I complained more than he ever did. Each time I would see Bob and ask him how he was doing, there was always the same answer: "I'm doing good!"

Every time we would sing "Through the Fire," I would look down from the stage at him sitting in his wheelchair, often with a big smile on his face. Tears would fill my eyes as I watched him. Many times I found myself asking, "God, why does such a good man have to go through all of that suffering?" I could never really find the answer and still haven't.

Bob was born August 7, 1955, in Idder, Alabama, in a church parsonage; his dad was the pastor of the church. The Reverend Bain had four children: three boys and one girl, with Bob being the youngest. They moved quite often, going from church to church and state to state. By the time Bob was twenty-one, his Dad had pastored twelve churches in three different states: Kentucky, Illinois, and Alabama.

The first three years of Bob's life were very normal. He was the baby and a PK (preacher's kid), which earned him a lot of attention and spoiling. Everyone with children should be able to remember the terrible two's. It is that age when the little ones are so inquisitive and wanting to explore everything. Bob started as a normal active two-year-old, but as he got closer to three, things began to change. Instead of all the energy that children usually have, he seemed to be drained, always worn down, and sleeping more than normal.

On his third birthday he became very sick and fell into a state of unconsciousness. Fear and panic gripped the hearts of the family as they rushed their almost lifeless child to the Pineville Community Hospital in Pineville, Kentucky. What had started out as a joyous birthday celebration ended at the emergency room.

No one had any idea what had happened to the little guy. They were praying and begging God to spare the life of their three-year-old son. The report from the doctor was that if he made it through the night, he might have a chance of survival. It was a touch-and-go situation all night.

The next day he gradually began to show signs of improvement. It was determined that he had gone into a diabetic coma. Little three-year-old Bob had to begin taking insulin by injection. After a two-week stay in the hospital, they returned home. All at once life had changed; a giant that he would battle for the rest of his life had attacked him.

In spite of his disease, he lived a relatively normal childhood. He rode bicycles, played basketball, and did things most boys his age did. Rickey, his older brother, spoke of several occasions when his little brother's sugar would drop, and it would cause him to behave in a manner completely opposite of his normal behavior. For instance, as he and others would play basketball, Bob would pick fights with the older boys. Big brother would have to jump in and bail him out of trouble.

Bob loved all sports, but his favorite was football. It was his dream to play on the school team. He tried out once, but due to his health problems, he was unable to make the team. When he was offered a position as a water boy, however, he gladly accepted. He felt it was the closest thing to being a team player.

As a teenager Bob became very interested in church. He was converted at age sixteen and baptized by his father in Springfield, Illinois. Soon afterward, he and a couple of his friends, Jim Austin and Cheryl Thrasher, formed a trio, singing Christian music. They called themselves the Ray of Hope Trio.

Bob was very serious about his work for the Lord, but he also loved to have lighthearted moments with his friends.

They traveled locally in the Illinois area, singing at churches and revival meetings.

In 1974 at the age of eighteen, Bob began his ministry and preached his first sermon at his dad's church. After that he never slowed down. He had found his calling in life—ministering the gospel.

In 1976 Bob married, and two years later he and his wife were blessed with a son. After ten years the marriage failed and ended in divorce. As devastating as that was, however, Bob never gave up. He held on to the belief that God was a God of forgiveness. He also knew that according to the scriptures, "For the gifts and the calling of God are without repentance" (Romans 11:29, KJV). He knew that he had the call of God on his life to proclaim the gospel message.

The following year he took a sabbatical. During that time he sought the support of his faithful friend and pastor, Joey Turman, at the Idder Church of God. With such good spiritual counsel and support from his pastor and friends, it wasn't long before Bob began to step back into his calling of ministering the gospel of salvation to all who were willing to hear.

He had always believed and preached that God was a God of forgiveness and mercy, but it was during this trying time in his own life that he found that belief to be so true. Now that he had experienced such an encounter with God's love, he was more determined than ever to go after others who were bruised and wounded, offering them the same message of restoration he had received.

In 1988, as a result of diabetes, Bob lost sight in his right eye. He later said, "The pain was almost unbearable." For several days all he could do was lie face down. Ahead of him, there were many more trials Bob was yet to face.

It was just five years later, April 19, 1993, on a Monday morning when Bob awakened to the horrible realization that he was blind in both eyes. He had already accepted the fact he was going to have to go through life with partial vision. But now he was going to have to cope with being totally blind. On the previous night, Bob had been in a revival in Middlesboro, Kentucky, where God had revealed Himself in a powerful way. It seemed almost impossible that things could take such a drastic turn in such a short time. It brought frustration and so many unanswered questions. "Why had God allowed it?"

His parents took him to the hospital in Harlan, Kentucky, where the doctors told them there was nothing they could do for him. Arrangements were made for him to go to the University of Kentucky hospital in Lexington, Kentucky. Two physicians performed a thorough examination. After receiving the results, one of the doctors sat on a stool beside Bob's bed and sadly stated, "Mr. Bain, you will never see again."

His mother and father could barely hold back the tears as they listened to the heartbreaking report. They didn't want to leave Bob alone, but with their minds and bodies completely exhausted, they left the hospital and checked in at a motel to try to get some rest. Mr. and Mrs. Bain slept very little, but rather spent most of their time crying, praying, and sending out prayer requests to friends and family on behalf of their son.

Bob's parents returned to the hospital about 7:00 a.m. the next day. Shortly afterward, a third physician, who had just been assigned to the case, came in to speak with them. He asked the other doctors, "Is this the man you wanted me to see?" They said, "Yes." Then he looked at Bob and asked, "Can you see?" Bob replied, "I can read your name tag." Everyone was amazed at such a turnaround. One of the doctors later told him, "It wasn't anything we did."

As Bob later spoke about the event, he talked about how he had prayed and questioned God during the time he was diagnosed with total blindness. He didn't understand how God expected him to preach if he couldn't even read his Bible. Then he said when he woke up, his sight had been miraculously restored to his left eye. After that he felt more compelled than ever to preach the gospel.

Two years later, in 1995, he faced yet another setback. Due to the toll that diabetes had taken upon his body, he was forced to go on dialysis three times a week. His niece, who has also been a diabetic since age four, recalled being with her uncle after one of his trips for dialysis. He looked broken-down and tired as she began to question him: "How do you do it? I need to know how you continue to fight and struggle to live. I am a diabetic, and I am petrified of what the future might hold for me."

Bob looked at her and said, "If I can tell one more person about Jesus, or if I can help lead one more soul to Christ, then the burden I have to bear on earth is nothing—especially compared to the Cross Christ bore at Calvary."

Even though his "outward man" was perishing, and his life was filled with doom and gloom, the "inward man" was being renewed with every word he spoke. So with words bubbling forth from that fountain of joy deep within, he continued: "If I can be an example to one more person of His mercy and grace, it will be worth it, for one day I am going to lay this old body down, and I won't have to suffer anymore."

He also testified that because he had to go to the clinic for dialysis, he was given the opportunity to come into contact with people he wouldn't ordinarily meet. Therefore it gave him an opportunity to witness to them about God's grace and mercy. He said that perhaps some of them would accept Jesus Christ as their Lord and Savior. He further testified, "As long as I have a chance to live, I have a chance to witness about the man who gave His life for this world, and that's what keeps me going."

In July 1999, Bob experienced another ravaging attack upon his body as severe pains gripped his chest. He received triple-bypass heart surgery the next day at Memorial Hospital in Chattanooga, Tennessee. Because of the damage to his arteries from the disease, once again his chance for survival looked very slim. But to everyone's amazement, he went home three days earlier than expected.

Thank God for the blessings that come to us even in the midst of the storms. In 1997 at the Church of God in Henagar, Alabama, Bob met a very special lady, Dianne. She had known him for a while, and in spite of his many physical complications, she felt God had put them together. I can personally testify that she was God-sent to my friend. Bob and Dianne were married October 22, 2000. Over the next four years she would prove to be a faithful companion and friend, and together they would journey through the darkest trials of their lives.

By 2001, Bob's already weak and frail body began to suffer even more from the effects of the devastating diabetes that had ravaged his body since childhood. Yet, this disease showed no mercy, as it cut off the blood circulation in his right leg; the doctors sadly informed Bob that the leg would have to be amputated. Even though this would be a major setback to Bob and his ministry, his faith never wavered.

Dianne once shared with me some of her and Bob's most memorable moments. She told me about the time when her husband was sitting in his recliner watching TV, and he looked at her and said, "I miss my first love."

Terribly confused by what he had said, her reply was, "What?"

He said it again: "I miss my first love."

She once again asked him what he was talking about, and he said, "I miss pastoring." Dianne could detect the deep longing in Bob's voice as he continued. "I would give anything if I could pastor a church again."

Dianne responded with caution because she didn't want to create false hope, yet she didn't want to crush her husband's dreams. So with a lot of apprehension she said, "Maybe after your leg heals and you regain your strength, God will allow you to pastor again."

Previously Bob had served on the Church of God State Music Committee, ministered as an evangelist, and pastored churches in three different cities: Bowling Green, Mount Washington, and Harlan, Kentucky. Many who had interacted with this man of God through the years knew that he had a pastor's heart. In spite of his own physical needs, he was always ready and willing to hasten to the aid of others in need.

Two weeks after their discussion about pastoring, Bob received a phone call from a minister, asking if he would be interested in filling in as pastor of a little church in Mount Pleasant, Tennessee. "Maybe you can help them get back on their feet," the minister stated.

Bob looked at Dianne and began to cry, so filled with emotions of joy he could barely speak. His response was, "My wife and I will talk it over and pray about it, and then I will get back with you in a few days."

Dianne was overjoyed that Bob had received the call, but also she was afraid that he wasn't physically able to take on the responsibilities of a pastor. He was very excited and asked Dianne what her thoughts were on the matter. Careful not to reveal all of her thoughts, she told him the decision about the church was for him to make. She concluded by saying, "All I can be is your wife and go wherever you feel like we need to be."

Two weeks later Bob went to the church in Mount Pleasant to meet the congregation and preach to them. The congregation voted him in as their pastor that day. Dianne said that if you had been sitting in the church with your eyes closed on that first Sunday, you would have never known that the powerful message you were hearing was coming from a very handicapped man sitting in a wheelchair.

Bob took on the new challenge as a man on a divine mission.

He was overjoyed that they had chosen him as their pastor; it was as though he had been given a new life. He felt that this church was where he was supposed to be. To him, the sky was the limit. His vision for the church was great, and he set out to accomplish it one soul at a time. There was a lot of work to be done, and though his body was weak, his spirit was strong; he was ready for the challenge.

In spite of his many physical handicaps, great things were happening in his ministry. For instance, one Sunday morning someone had invited three sisters to church who had drifted from their Christian faith and had not been to church for quite a while. That Sunday morning, when Bob preached and gave the invitation, all three sisters came and renewed their commitment to Christ. It was a glorious day as the whole congregation rejoiced together.

As well as being a faithful pastor to his already established congregation, Bob was continually trying to get new people to come to church. Dianne said that he would come out of dialysis ready to go visit a sick or shut-in church member. She would ask, "Don't you think we should go home and rest first?"

He would answer, "I'll be all right; I'll rest tonight."

She later said, "I believe God gave my husband one last chance to pastor again, so he could prove to God and to himself that he had given his all." He did just that and never once complained.

The church had previously purchased some land, with intentions of building a new sanctuary, but over the years the vision had grown dim. Pastor Bain brought new life to the old vision. The property was cleaned off and a new sign was erected in place of an old one that read, "Future Home of Living Waters Church."

One Sunday, a service was held on the grounds where a tent had been erected. It was the very spot where they hoped one day to build a new church sanctuary. There was much excitement as a large crowd gathered to hear Pastor Bain preach. Those who attended the service said that it was one of the best sermons he had ever preached. That Sunday an even greater excitement gripped Bob, and he looked with great anticipation to the future of their church.

Yet, just a few days after that victorious tent service, it was as if someone flipped a switch, and what little bit of good health he had left was taken. During this time his memory would come and go, and it became a struggle for him to simply study the Bible.

Just a short time after this most recent attack upon his body, he once again lost the vision in his left eye. After blindness set in, it became difficult for Bob to minister. Dianne tried to assist him as much as she could by reading his text for him, but it was so different from what he had been accustomed to. With his body so broken and with the frustration of not being able to read on his own, it became almost too much for him to bear. He felt he had nothing left to give.

The happiest Dianne had ever seen her husband was when he was pastoring the little church in Mount Pleasant. She knew, however, it was just a matter of time until that, too, would be taken from him.

One Sunday morning she could tell that he had something very heavy weighing on his mind. Therefore, she was not surprised when he told her that he was going to have to give the church up. He said his health made it impossible for him to be the pastor the congregation needed and deserved. What a heart-wrenching moment it was for Bob and Dianne. She knew that he had given his all, but he was unable to continue.

Dianne shared her husband's sadness in having to give up the thing that he dearly loved—pastoring. She vividly remembered how her husband had referred to pastoring as his first love.

The following Sunday morning, Dianne stood with her hands on her husband's shoulder as he poured out his heart to the congregation. With tear-filled eyes and a broken heart, Pastor Bain announced his resignation. He told his congregation he was sorry that he was unable to do all he had hoped to do, but he was glad that God had given him one more opportunity to pastor. Dianne said that it was the hardest thing she had ever seen him have to do.

Two weeks later he preached his farewell message to his loving congregation. For twenty-three months he had put his heart and soul into the Mount Pleasant Church of God. Although the new building was never built, and his entire vision for his congregation never came to pass, he felt that he had completed the task of being a good and faithful servant.

After leaving the church, Bob's brother Ricky made arrangements for them to come and stay with him in his home in St. Peters, Missouri. This invitation to stay with his brother was such a blessing. With his health in such bad shape, Bob could do very little for himself, and it became almost impossible for Dianne to lift him without some kind of help.

Not long after they moved Bob began experiencing severe problems and pain with his other leg, which led to another amputation.

One day after living in his brother's home for fifteen months, Bob told Dianne, "I want to go home."

Her reply was, "We are at home."

He said, "No! I want to go back South."

A lot of preparations had to be made before they could move. She had to arrange for his dialysis. It took about a month to get everything set up.

After moving back, he began having complications with his leg that had most recently undergone amputation. As a result he had to undergo more surgery. Since it was almost impossible for his wife to transport him by herself, the couple desperately prayed for help.

In response to their prayer, the Idder Church of God stepped in and sponsored a fundraiser. With the proceeds they purchased a van designed with a lift and presented it to the Bain family. What an answer to prayer, and what a Christian thing to do. Since they now had a van with a lift in it, Dianne could transport Bob back and forth to dialysis by herself. Also, it was now much easier for him to attend church. Dianne said that he would go every time he was able to go.

About one month before Bob's passing, a friend and I went to visit him at his home in Trenton, Georgia. I had called ahead and told his wife that we wanted to surprise him. As we pulled into the driveway of their home, he was sitting on his porch in his wheelchair. I was shocked by the condition of my friend. There he sat in a wheelchair with both legs amputated, and blind in both eyes. He was the picture of death. My heart melted within me as I looked upon the horrible condition of my friend.

As we walked up to the porch, and I called out his name, a big smile came across his face as he recognized my voice. It was difficult to find the right words to say, so I just reached down and gave him a hug. Knowing I needed to speak, but unable to think of anything appropriate to say, I asked him how he was doing.

His reply was, as always, "I'm doing good."

During the whole visit, I never once heard him complain. He didn't bring up any of the horrible things that he had been through. Instead, he talked as if he were ready to hit the preaching trail again.

We had a wonderful visit as we talked and reminisced for about an hour. After that, I could tell our friend was getting worn down and tired, so we said our goodbyes. Before we left, we had prayer with him. I will never forget Bob's words as he prayed. He asked for God's blessings to be on us, and then he asked God to heal him.

As we were leaving, I gave Bob a DVD of The Crabb Family, *Live at Brooklyn Tabernacle*. I had always tried to keep him well stocked with our music. The recording contained the song "Through the Fire." Dianne said afterward that he would lie down and listen to it over and over.

I wasn't really surprised when I received a call asking if I would sing at Bob's funeral service. What an honor it was to be part of such a great memorial service. That man showed us how to get through the furnace of affliction with faith, with integrity, and with dignity.

On the morning of Bob's death he had suffered greatly and was very weak. At times he would become incoherent. Dianne shared with me the details of their final moments, brushing the tears from her eyes. She said that at approximately 10:00 a.m., he asked her to lie down beside him. He told her that he was sorry he had never been able to do as much for her as she had done for him. With a very weak and trembling voice, he said that he hoped she knew how much he loved her. Unable to hold back the tears, she assured him that she knew. She said that conversation was the last one she and her beloved husband ever shared.

Dianne told me that in the few hours just before Bob's death, he seemed to be struggling to hold on. At about five that evening she leaned over to him and said, "Bob I know you're tired, and I know that you want to see 'Buster' (the nickname for his son, Ryan, who was on his way to visit him), but if you want to go on, he'll understand." She continued to assure Bob that she would be all right: "Even though it's gonna be hard, you must know that I'll be all right."

All Bob could do in response to his wife's words was to barely shake his head. She said, "It's okay; you don't have to hold on any longer if you don't want to. We're all gonna be okay."

The words Dianne spoke seemed to be the words he needed to hear, and on April 26, 2005, Bob's walk through the fire ended as he took his final breath and went home to be with the Lord.

Earlier that morning someone standing nearby heard Bob whisper, "I love you Lord." I will never understand why he went through the many, many trials that he did. It has been said many times, "the greater the test, the greater the testimony." What a testimony Bob Bain left behind. It will forever be etched in the minds of those who loved him and knew him well.

Chapter 5

So Many Times in Trials

Stephanie grew up in the Bluegrass state of Kentucky, surrounded by rolling hills, crops, farms, and acres and acres of hardwood timber. It was a beautiful place to live, where farmers helped each other in planting and harvesting crops, building barns, and other farm chores. It wasn't at all uncommon to pick someone up and give them a ride into town or to help other families with their children. That's just the way people did things back then.

Families would get together and play ball, sing, go on hayrides, and have cookouts, which often included fish fry's. Everybody just pulled together.

Church was no option; it was mandatory that they go. Services were held regularly on Sunday morning, Sunday night, Wednesday night, and other nights as well if there was a revival in the area. Stephanie's family attended the Baptist Church, yet fellowshipped with other denominations when they were having special meetings. Everybody basically knew each other, and their outlook was that they were all going to the same Heaven.

For six years Stephanie was an only child. Most of her days were filled with playing in her little-girl world of make-believe. She loved playing Mom with one of her many baby dolls. During her first year of school, she was blessed with a baby brother, Jeremy. She adjusted well with the *drastic* change of having most of the attention directed from her to the new baby. In the back of her childlike mind, she saw herself as now having a live baby doll. When no one was looking, she would dress him in her doll clothes and pretend he was her baby girl. Overnight she went from being everyone's little girl to being the big girl.

A couple of years later, just when she was getting used to having a brother, another baby brother, Matt, was born. Two years later, when she was age ten, she was blessed with yet another brother, named Jonathan. Stephanie vividly remembers riding the school bus home from school, while three little brothers waited impatiently at home for her arrival. At the sight of the big yellow bus, the little guys would run down the long driveway laughing, screaming, and tripping over their own feet. She always looked forward to their warm welcome. It made the long, grueling day at school seem worthwhile. They loved their big sister and were always happy when she got home.

"Steph" was more like a big brother, a tomboy. Her days of playing house and playing with baby dolls were over. She had other interests now, such as wrestling, climbing trees, throwing rocks, and playing in the mud. She had become quite a leader at helping these little guys get into all sorts of trouble. They all looked up to her as big sister, so it was very easy for her to convince them to do almost anything. She found it very amusing as she led them into mischievousness. It was especially funny when they would get into trouble and she wouldn't.

One day, after watching a program on TV about Pee-wee Herman ice-skating, she decided that they would go skating too. She poured a bucket of water on the floor in their house and added dish detergent, which made it very slippery. The four of them would run and slide into the furniture and walls. They were having the time of their lives, until Mom walked in and saw what they were doing and what a mess they had made. As Mom was cleaning up the mess, they were arguing over who had the largest bruises from slamming against the furniture.

On another occasion the four children were playing in a playhouse that Dad had built for them. All at once the field that surrounded their home and the playhouse was in flames. Everyone feared that their home was going to catch fire and be destroyed. Fortunately, the fire was subdued and everyone was safe. Steph later discovered that one of her little brothers had picked up a lighter from home and had set the field on fire. That bit of information remained a secret between the two of them.

After the boys got a little older, their parents purchased a couple of go-carts and built a track for them to ride on. One day while Steph and Jeremy were riding, they noticed their seven-year-old brother Matt standing near the track. Her suggestion was that they pretend they were going to run over him. Jeremy quickly agreed, and they both burst into laughter. They thought that it would be funny to scare him.

As they both drove toward Matt, Steph turned her steering wheel to miss him. But for some reason Jeremy's go-cart rolled right over Matt. As they rushed to him, they found him scratched and bleeding, with tire tracks on his face and chest. At first they thought he was dead; they were so relieved when he began to cry. Jeremy and Steph agreed they must tell the same story, which wasn't quite the truth. They told Mom and Dad that Matt walked right out in front of them.

To say their parents had their hands full with those four would be putting it mildly. They were continually getting into something, and big sister was usually the ringleader.

It wasn't too many years later when all the meanness that Steph had taught her brothers backfired on her. When the years of dating came around, there was nothing worse than having three little mean brothers to contend with. As she and her date would be standing outside of the home, the boys would tap on the windows and snicker at them. It was extremely embarrassing to her when her brothers would harass her boyfriend, whom she was trying to impress.

Steph wasn't allowed to wear makeup at home, but her grandmother would secretly give her cosmetics because she disagreed with the parents' decision. A couple of the brothers found where she had hid the makeup. At times they would climb up the big antique dresser and destroy or remove her makeup. She couldn't snitch on them since she wasn't supposed to have it in the first place.

But big sister figured out ways to get back at her brothers. She would take their Hot Wheels cars and other toys and bury them in the yard. She continued doing that for several months, never telling them what had happened to their toys, acting as though she had never seen them.

One day as Jeremy was climbing up to get into her things, he tipped the dresser over on himself. As she had her brother pinned between the dresser and bed screaming for help, all she could do was laugh. She allowed him to stay there for a while, thinking he wasn't going to get out.

Through their years at home together as a family, the children were very close. They laughed together, fought together, played together, and most of all, prayed together. Life wasn't perfect; there were many bumps in the road along the way. But through it all, love always prevailed.

Over the years, life's choices, opportunities, and responsibilities led them in many different directions, putting a strain on the closeness that once existed. Christmas, Birthdays, and special occasions were about the only times when Stephanie and her original family could get together as a family. This was due to being so tied up with the demands of every day life.

One day while Stephanie was running late for work, a guy in a white truck cut her off in traffic. As he pulled in front of her, he slowed down, blowing his horn and waving at her. She thought he was out of his mind. She wasn't too happy about the whole situation. As she pulled in to where she worked, he turned around and followed her in.

"I thought I had seen an angel," he said, "but now I know I have seen one." All Stephanie could do was smile and say, "You're sweet."

For the next thirty days, every day, she received one dozen roses and a teddy bear. They were delivered to the office where she worked. After a few days it looked like a funeral home or a florist's shop. The man would often call Stephanie at work or come by. His persistence was resisted for about six months, then after finding an ink pen on her desk with his work number on it, she decided to give him a call. She realized she was attracted to him. From that day forward she and John McGinnis were inseparable. It was very obvious that they were in love. Perhaps, by way of the broken road, it had been destiny that brought them together.

It wasn't long into their relationship until they were faced with some major trials. To make it through, they would need to depend on strength, love, and support from each other and from God.

Upon spending time together, Stephanie and John were so excited about their new life. Days and nights were filled with laughter and joy. They would talk for hours about their plans for the future. She especially liked to talk about their upcoming wedding; it almost felt like a fairytale love story.

One day while at work John received a call from his twelve-year-old niece. With panic in her voice, she began to scream, "I can't wake up Mom. She is lying on the floor, and I can't wake her up." He knew from the sound of her voice and by the feeling in the pit of his stomach that something was terribly wrong.

Within a short while it was confirmed that his oldest sister was dead at age thirty-three. Later, an autopsy showed that she had died from an overdose of prescription drugs.

John felt so helpless. He was at least seventeen hundred miles away from his sister's family. It was like everything just came crashing down. So many questions flooded his mind as he asked himself over and over, "What could I have done that would have made a difference?"

John suffered a mental and physical breakdown, which was to last for several months.

With John being unable to supervise his construction company, it ran into financial troubles. He was forced to lay off his employees.

John was unable to eat or sleep properly. He suffered with stomach complications that were very painful at times. He would often run a high temperature; he would sometimes black out or become incoherent. It was a battle that he could have never fought alone. Stephanie became his rock; she was determined to pull him through.

Even in the midst of such trying times, they still felt that they should continue with the wedding plans. It was scheduled to take place at a small country church in Central Kentucky.

Stephanie had always been very close to her brother Jeremy, and she really wanted him to participate in the ceremony, but he was reluctant to make any promises. He did not like dressing up in a suit. He was a country boy; he liked fishing, hunting, jeans, and boots.

The first time John and Jeremy met, John was doing some reconstruction on his future mother-in-law's house. Jeremy's favorite dog had been struck and killed by a vehicle; he was heartbroken. He picked the dog up out of the road and carried it to the house. Feeling very sorry for young Jeremy, who was about seventeen, John asked, "Would you like me to bury him for you?"

"No," Jeremy answered, "there are some things a man has to do for himself."

Usually Jeremy was very serious, but at times he revealed his humorous side. One day he was teasing his sister and asked her, "What is it about me that makes all the girls want me? Is it my money? Is it my muscles? (He was small for his age.) Is it my car? (He had worked hard and paid for a dark blue Camaro.) Or is it my baby face?" They all got a good laugh out of that.

On the day of the wedding, a few friends and family members had begun to arrive, but Jeremy was absent. The soon-to-be-bride had sadly accepted that her brother wasn't going to show up.

Just a few minutes before it was time to begin, however, he pulled up in his sports car. He got out in jeans and boots, sporting a black eye that he had received from a scuffle he'd had the night before. He walked in, to where his sister and the other girls were making their last minute preparations, and said, "Steph, I didn't want to come, but you know how I am, I did what I was supposed to." She was in tears, but they were tears of joy at seeing him, black eye and all. They had a laugh about his black eye, and then he left to carry out his duties in the ceremony. He lit the candles and escorted his mom and his grandmother to their seats.

The wedding was small and simple, but it was a beautiful event. John wore a white tuxedo with a dark vest and bow tie, and on his lapel was pinned a wine-colored rose bud. He was a very handsome groom. Stephanie wore a long white wedding gown and veil. She carried a bouquet of white- and wine-colored roses. She was a beautiful bride with her long blond wavy hair and sparkling green eyes. It was a great day! It was just months after the death of John's sister and it brought the two of them some much needed joy. John and Stephanie were finally husband and wife.

Money was tight due to John's sickness, so they spent their honeymoon at his apartment. They couldn't have been any more content if they had been staying at the Ritz-Carlton.

They were now a *blended* family—John, Stephanie, and her little three-year old daughter Mattie. Even though John was still having a very difficult time struggling with the death of his sister, they were determined to make it through the storm and have peace and tranquility in their lives again.

Stephanie took the role of helping John through his breakdown, which proved to be a real test of love on her part. At the time they married, he was a very weak man, mentally and physically. There was no guarantee that he would ever be that jolly, happy guy that she had fallen in love with. Before the breakdown, he was continually trying to make her smile. There was no guarantee that he would be able to work and provide for her and Mattie, yet love prevailed, and she took a chance.

About eight months into their marriage they had taken a trip to Georgia. Upon their returning, they stopped by her grandparents' house to check on them. They were somewhat shocked to find no one at home; fear gripped both of them as they walked to her aunt's house nearby. Her aunt met them in the yard. "Where is everyone?" Stephanie asked her.

"Haven't they told you?" was her aunt's reply. At that time Stephanie thought that her grandfather had gotten sick or something.

"Is it Grandpa?" she continued.

"No," her aunt said. "Jeremy has been in a very bad car wreck and they are not expecting him to live."

After hearing the horrible news Stephanie collapsed and fell to the ground. They carried her limp body into the house and revived her, but when she once again became conscious, she found that the horrible news she had heard was no bad dream; it was the truth. Late into the night Jeremy had lost control of his car. As his vehicle left the road, it hit a tree, throwing him from the car. The car then rolled over him. A friend who was passing by found his broken body.

He was taken by ambulance to the hospital in Louisville, Kentucky. He was in a horrible condition. His brain was swollen, he was bleeding internally, and many of his bones were crushed. Family members were told upon their arrival that Jeremy would probably be dead in two hours. He was so bruised and swollen that he was unrecognizable. Some of the family members began to pray, asking God to spare his life and give them a miracle.

Jeremy pulled through the night, which gave them hope. The next day, the doctor did a craniotomy, a neurosurgical procedure in which a piece of the skull is removed, allowing expansion room for a swelling brain. Jeremy was covered with wires and braces. He was in traction and was hooked to all sorts of monitors and IV tubes.

To look at him, you would say there is no way this young man would be able to survive. Hours turned into days, days turned into weeks, and weeks turned into months. He underwent brain surgery and many bone reconstruction surgeries. Every week it was something new. After a couple of months the doctors felt confident that he was going to pull through, but he was facing a very long road of rehabilitation.

Two months after the wreck, Stephanie gave birth to a little girl, whom they named Star. In the midst of all the pain, Star was a ray of sunshine.

To say that Stephanie was a very strong young lady would be putting it mildly. God had endowed her with His grace and strength, therefore enabling her to keep everything together, even when it seemed impossible.

Jeremy was a fighter. There were numerous trips to therapy and rehab centers. He basically had to learn to do everything all over again. He soon discovered that things as simple as opening and closing his hand to make a fist, bending his knees, speaking a sentence, or counting from one to ten were all major tasks. It was like a small child learning a little day by day.

Each new feat achieved was a celebration. Due to the severity of the damage to his brain, it did not function as a normal twenty-three-year-old brain. It now functioned as that of a child. The therapy did advance Jeremy in his mental capacity, but it was a slow process. Within a few weeks of the wreck, he was classified as completely disabled. The physicians agreed that it would be many months before he would be able to hold down any type of job, and most likely, never. It would turn out that over five years, his evaluation progressed mentally from that of a young child to that of a twelve-year-old.

The more Jeremy progressed, the harder it was for him to sit still. After a year, he had gone without working about as long as he could; he needed something to do that made him feel helpful.

He made a trip to the Social Security office and informed them that he was not disabled and did not want their check or any other handouts.

He began putting in job applications and trying to find someone who would let him work.

After several weeks of searching, and with no hope in sight of finding work, he bought a John Deere riding lawnmower and began mowing yards. He would work for many hours doing lawn work. This would leave him with excruciating pain, but he never complained. He was glad to be able to work. There were many times when he would mow yards for the elderly and would take no money from them.

One day he was doing some work at the house where he had grown up. While digging a trench in his yard, he began to uncover toys. It was his Hot Wheels cars and other toys that had mysteriously disappeared so many years ago. He knew exactly who the culprit was; he went straight to show Stephanie what he had found. He knew from the guilty look on her face that she was the one who had sneaked and buried them to hide them from him and his brothers. It was a hilarious moment.

John and Stephanie were in the process of purchasing their first home. Although there would be a lot of work involved with remodeling, they were very excited. For the first four years they had been married, they had lived in an apartment and a rental house, but finally they were going to put their money into something that would be theirs.

It was a beautiful place on the outskirts of town. It had a large front yard—a great place for the children to play. The view from the backyard was breathtaking, with rolling hills and a creek running through the countryside.

It was a two-story house; the outside was done in Bedford stone. The living room had a large rock fireplace that was beautiful. John had spent several months remodeling the interior of the home, and there was still a ways to go. But it was a labor of love for his family, and he was happy that they were going to have a place to call home.

One day, after they had been living in the house for only a couple of months, John and one of his employees were working out in the yard, when John heard his employee scream, "Your house is on fire!" John quickly got the water hose and ran toward the house, but when he opened the door, the force of the fire knocked him to the ground.

In the meantime, Stephanie and the two girls had gone to enroll Mattie in school. They had been gone about twenty minutes when her mother reached her on the phone and said, "Someone called me and said they heard on the scanner that your house was on fire."

Stephanie replied, "I know that's not right; we just left a few minutes ago and everything was fine." But she returned home to find that it was very true. Her house was almost completely gone.

When the fire was over, the house and everything in it was a total loss. It's a very strange experience when that happens. Before the fire, you may feel like you don't have a lot of things, but when you see them in ashes, you realize how precious your possessions were. It's a horrible feeling; it feels almost like a death.

The couple had paid a forty-thousand-dollar down payment that was in an escrow account, but they had no homeowner's insurance on the house. Therefore, everything was a total loss.

Among the blackened ruins was a very special blanket that Stephanie's grandmother had made for Star when she was born. It had become Star's security blanket. She had held on to it, slept with it, and dragged it around for three years. Star cried for several days and found it very difficult to sleep without her blanket.

For the young family, it was time to start over again. Four years prior to this horrible incident, they had lost everything in financial troubles; now they found themselves going through yet another trial. Through it all they were learning to be survivors and fighters.

Money sometimes appeared in unexpected places. John signed up for a fishing tournament a few weeks after the house had burned. The tournament was held near Louisville, Kentucky. It was to help benefit the Muscular Dystrophy Association. There were nearly two hundred entries in the tournament.

John finished in first place and won $10,000. He also won the Big Fish Money; it was over $4,000. Big Fish Money is where each fisherman puts in a certain amount, and the fisherman who catches the biggest fish gets the money. Though they were in desperate need of money to help them get a house and furnishings for a house, John never gave it a second thought: He immediately donated some money to the MDA fund. He is a very giving person.

After the fire, the McGinnis family moved into a motel. This move proved to be very expensive, and they found their funds were quickly running out. There was only one option left; move into the bait shop that they operated.

The bait shop and game room was a place where the local fishermen would stop in and tell their fishing stories and pick up some bait or fishing tackle. It was also a hangout where people would get together, play a game of pool, listen to the jukebox, and drink a Coke.

It was not a big business; it was more of a hobby. But since John was in the construction business and construction was slow, the bait shop and game room helped to supplement their income.

The bait shop was definitely not set up with family quarters. It shared the rest room with another business. It was equipped with a commode and a sink. Dishes were washed in a bucket, supper was cooked on a hot plate, and Hamburger Helper was served almost every night. One of the pool tables was used as the dining table. Baths were taken the old-fashioned way, with a washcloth and a bucket or pan of warm water. It was an open building; therefore, the living room was open to the public.

The McGinnis family couldn't close down the shop because they needed the revenue, so it had to serve as both a business and a living space. They were between a rock and a hard place, but they made do with what they had. In the meantime they had bought a piece of land a few miles away.

John used his building experience and began building a house for his family. He worked long hours, sometimes twelve and fourteen hours a day, often by himself. He was determined to get his family out of the make-do home, the bait shop, and into a real home.

During this time Jeremy had made much progress since his accident. He had gone from doing therapy every weekday for two straight years to once again being able to drive. Yet he still wasn't out of the woods. He was told that one fall the wrong way could leave him paralyzed for life. But that didn't slow him down.

Throughout the many hours of being housebound, he had become a huge fan of western movies and John Wayne. After he had recovered to the point of getting around on his own, the "cowboy" inside him wanted to ride a horse. Someone he knew allowed him to get up on his horse, even after being warned of what could happen in case of a severe fall. But Jeremy did it anyway. The horse threw him off; he just sat and laughed about it, then got up, brushed himself off, and went on his way.

Even though Jeremy had to deal with severe pain, he still fought and pushed himself hard. He was continually troubled because he couldn't seem to get back to his old self. He spoke openly to his sister about his feelings. He was self-conscious that people thought he was ugly, and that people thought he was mentally unstable.

He had come so far—from sitting in a wheelchair shaking uncontrollably, to driving a car and doing some light work. But every day was a challenge and most days were filled with frustration.

One afternoon Jeremy came by to visit with John and Stephanie. He knocked on the door, and his sister came to the door. "Who is your company?" he asked. He seemed very disturbed because of their visitor. It upset his sister because his actions seemed so rude. He refused to go in; he just got in his truck and drove away. Stephanie was very troubled; she could tell that Jeremy just wasn't himself. He had acted very strangely. She had no idea what had upset him.

About fifteen minutes later, someone knocked on the door. It was her brother's friend. Stephanie could tell something was wrong by the look on his face. He said to her, "Jeremy is dead. He has shot himself; he's dead." She and her middle brother, Matt, fell to the floor and began praying.

As they later arrived at the house where the shooting had taken place, there were several police cars and an ambulance. It was like a bad dream; it didn't feel like it could really be happening. Stephanie got out of their vehicle and was making her way to the scene of the incident when a friend stopped her. He held her down and said to her, "You trust me, don't you?"

"Yes," she replied.

He said, "You can't go in there."

She turned around and remained outside. She saw Jonathan, her youngest brother, who had witnessed the shooting. He was sitting on the curb screaming, "He didn't mean to; he didn't mean to."

The body was placed in the ambulance and taken away. The family, soon afterward, went to the police department. There they were informed that Jeremy had died as a result of a gunshot to the head. Stephanie was given her brother's wallet. As she opened it, she found a picture of her and her two daughters that she had given him. She also saw his GED card that she had helped him obtain; he had been so proud of that.

Stephanie could not hold back the tears as many memories filled her mind.

Most of the family spent the night at her mother's house. It was a horrible night.

Everyone was devastated. Jonathan and his father had witnessed the shooting. Jonathan kept saying over and over, "He didn't mean to do it. If you could have seen the look on his face, he didn't mean to do it." He felt that Jeremy was just upset about something. When he would get upset, it would be extreme. This behavior was due to his brain injury.

Before the shooting took place, Jeremy had been carrying a .44 Magnum pistol that he had owned for several years. He was waving it around, pointing it at himself saying, "No one loves me."

Jonathan was persistent as he once again said, "He didn't really want to hurt himself or anyone else. He was just upset and trying to get their attention."

That terrible night was when the torment began. Stephanie couldn't sleep. When she would close her eyes, she would see horrible images of Jeremy. She was overtaken with fear.

The day of the viewing she prayed before going into the funeral home, begging God for strength. For the first time she received some peace. Deep inside she kept hearing, "God is a just God."

It was a closed-casket funeral with many beautiful flowers. The love and comfort from those who attended was overwhelming and very much needed for Stephanie and her family to get through such a devastating time.

Life for Stephanie then drastically changed. Everything had become a blur. All the joy in life had been taken from her. She knew it wasn't fair for her husband and two daughters that she wasn't giving them the love and attention they needed. But it was beyond her control. When she would hear someone knock at the door, she feared that if she opened the door it would be her brother standing there wounded and bleeding. Often she would visualize him as a young child playing around her; it seemed so realistic.

Three months after the death of her brother, she found that she was pregnant. For a while she was very disturbed. When they told her the baby was a boy, it was somewhat of a consolation. After John lost his sister, God gave them a baby girl, and now after losing her brother, God was giving them a baby boy. That day brought some joy, but it was short-lived. The nightmares continued night after night. She would look in the mirror and see her brother looking back at her. Nights were especially bad. She feared if she looked out into the darkness she would see him in his wounded condition.

Every day was filled with many questions in her mind: "Why didn't I do this or that? Why didn't I do something different?"

The torment continued throughout the term of her pregnancy. She gave birth to a beautiful baby boy. They named him River. He was born one year after Jeremy had died. Though the family had been blessed with a beautiful baby boy, Stephanie's mental torment was as bad as it ever was.

Within five years they had gone from being financially secure to being broke twice, and losing a house and all personal belongings to a fire. A further challenge had been the death of her sister-in-law and the mental and physical breakdown of her husband that lasted for over a year. After that was the car wreck of her brother and his long recovery. Just when she thought things had to get better, she had to experience the horrible tragedy of her brother's violent death.

John had worked relentlessly to pay the bills, to feed his family, and to finish the house. Stephanie had kept most of her feelings to herself. She lived in her own personal nightmare. And no one, not even her husband, knew the severity of her mental anguish. Looking back, she was possibly suffering from postpartum depression along with depression brought about by the traumatic experiences she had endured.

For the last five years she had been a solid rock for her family. But she had reached a breaking point and didn't feel that she could handle it anymore.

One day while driving along, she was trying to pull her thoughts together. There had been no relief from the nightmares, sleepless nights, and dreaded fear of another horrible mental vision. She was ready for it to end. As she drove she saw a large tree on the side of the road. Her intentions were to slam her car into the tree at a high rate of speed and end her nightmare.

Just as she built enough determination to end her life, a song came on the radio that said, "So many times I've questioned certain circumstances and things I could not understand."

Those words caught her attention and she pulled the car over to the side of the road. She wept and prayed as she continued listening to the rest of the song, "Through the Fire."

While still in tears, she returned home and said to her husband, "I am going to make it." Together they knelt down and begin to pray, asking God for help. Everything began to change, and a healing began to take place in her mind.

Afterward when she would sense any sign of depression returning, she would ask her husband to sing "Through the Fire," and the dark cloud would seem to lift.

Today the McGinnis family lives on a hundred-and-fifty-acre farm with four lakes heavily stocked with bass fish. They live in a beautiful thirty-nine-hundred square foot house. They own a construction company that employs twenty to thirty-five employees during the peak season. John is a pro fisherman with FLW Outdoors, with several winnings under his belt. Among many other major sponsors, Hardee's sponsors him.

They are a very devoted Christian family. John enjoys singing, songwriting, and speaking at local churches. They enjoy lots of family time and especially enjoy visits from pap pa Dorsey.

Sometimes when John is off on a fishing trip, Stephanie has what is called a "day of just play" with the children. They dress up and do all kind of fun things that kids like to do. They wreck the house and just before Dad returns they hurry to clean everything up.

One day, a few summers after Jeremy's death, John and Stephanie were planting flowers under a tree. As John was digging, he discovered something buried in the dirt. He removed it and brushed it. They realized that it was a stuffed Disney Goofy doll that had been missing for a few years. Immediately, Stephanie saw a mental picture of Jeremy laughing. It brought a tearful smile to her face; she knew who the culprit was.

What a blessing it has been for me to know this beautiful family and to see how God has brought them through so many trials.

Stephanie has told me, "Your song, 'Through the Fire,' saved my life."

And several times John has said to me, "I have a wife today and my children have a mother because of the song 'Through the Fire.'" Once again I am amazed at the tools God uses to complete his miraculous work of grace.

I feel very humbled to have held the pen.

Chapter 6

Help Will Always Come in Time

"The first time I heard the song 'Through the Fire,' I was ten years old. I got so excited; I wanted to get up and start preaching." Those are the words of Luke Armbrister, recalling the summer of 2000. The Crabb Family was in revival in Muskogee, Oklahoma. We were singing, and I was the evangelist. Luke and his family came to Muskogee to be in the revival. They had driven sixty miles from their hometown of Claremore, Oklahoma.

At the time, our radio single was "Through the Fire." The song was getting quite a bit of radio airplay, yet many of people who attended the revival were hearing the song for the first time. As Luke and his family listened to the song that night, they had no idea how drastically Luke's life was to change a few months later, and how the words of that song would impact their lives.

Luke was born on February 9, 1989, to Jeff and Karen Armbrister. He has two sisters, Samantha and Celeste. Ever since Luke could remember, his dad worked very hard in construction and also traveled as an evangelist conducting revivals and helping out pastors. Not only did Luke's parents dedicate their son to God and instill within him a faith and love for God, they also took it a step further as they demonstrated a faith and love for God in their everyday lives.

At a very young age, Luke would take part in singing at the church services. By the age of four, he became interested in playing the drums.

Since his legs were too short to reach the bass drum pedal, he would thump the top of the pedal with his toe. Though he was small, he was very persistent, and by the time he was eleven years old he was an accomplished drummer. During this time he had also become interested in the guitar and the bass guitar and had set out to master them as well.

For Luke's entire life he and his family have lived in Claremore, Oklahoma. The town is about thirty miles northeast of Tulsa. It is best known as having been the home to Will Rogers, who was an actor and writer in the early 1900s. Other notable residents include Garth Brooks and Patti Page. Claremore was also the town that inspired the award-winning musical *Oklahoma*. It's a friendly little western town of about seventeen thousand people.

Although he was raised in a Christian home and had accepted Jesus Christ as his Lord and Savior by age eight, Luke was still 100 percent boy. For instance, one Sunday afternoon a couple of his friends from church went home with him to visit until the evening service. Trying to come up with something to do, they decided to get the BB gun and do some target practice. Luke's grandfather owned a field in which several old bread delivery trucks, vans, and buses were kept. His grandfather and one of his uncles owned the vehicles. The boys' targets became the windshields, taillights, headlights, mirrors, and the radiators of the vehicles. When all the fun was over, he said that there was not one breakable thing left on most of those vehicles that was not broken. All but two of the vehicles had received extreme damage. Not only did he find himself in trouble with his dad, but his grandfather and uncle were quite upset with him as well.

Another boyish prank involved chicken eggs. Luke's grandpa always kept chickens around so that they could have fresh eggs. One day when Luke was about eight years old, he found some eggs under his mother's porch steps that had been there for quite some time; he gathered the eggs and carried them to his uncle's house nearby. He threw every one of the rotten eggs near the front door. When his uncle got home from work—as Luke put it—"he was hot." He made his little mischievous nephew clean up the mess he had made with the rotten eggs.

Luke's dad and the father of one of his best friends were board members of one of the Holiness Church youth camps in Oklahoma. The chairman of the board was his friend's grandfather. Luke said that by the age of nine he and his friend had acquired the reputation of being the most mischievous two boys to ever attend that youth camp.

At one particular youth camp the boys got into some serious mischief. They became aware of the whereabouts of some confiscated fireworks that had been taken away from them and other campers. The fireworks were being securely kept in his grandfather's office. One day while the office was vacant the two boys slipped in and took the fireworks. Luke and his buddy then took the fireworks to a room above the girl's dorm. As the girls came out of their dorm, they became unexpected targets for the two mischievous boys who aimed bottle rockets at them and threw firecrackers in an attempt to scare them.

Luke's motto was, and still is, "Life is only as fun as what you make it, so I try to make the best of it." Because of his playful and spirited attitude, Luke had to be disciplined quite often. After chastising him, his parents would explain to him the error of his ways, and since he had such a sensitive nature, his prayer of "Lord, I'm sorry" would often follow. Yet underneath all the mischief and youthful energy, this little fellow had a deep-rooted love for Jesus Christ and enjoyed going to church as much as anybody.

The Armbrister guys were serious hunters, especially for deer. Jeff, his dad, was a very skillful hunter, and he started teaching his son how to hunt at a very early age. As proof of just how serious these guys take hunting, Luke's parents have a picture of their son with an orange hunting vest wrapped around him, pinned with a safety pin. It was his first hunting trip; he was only two years old.

November 18, 2000, is a day the Armbristers will never forget. Luke was eleven years old. It was the first day of deer season, and they were anxious to get into the woods. Prior to hunting season they had scouted out the place where they were going to hunt. They were ready to take down that trophy buck. Luke and his dad spent some quality father and son time together as they made their way into the woods. It was still dark that morning as they climbed into their stands, which were some distance from each other. As Jeff sat in the stand, he thought, "What a thrill it is for a father to watch his son bring down a deer, especially his first."

After a short while in the woods, Luke beeped his dad on the walkie-talkie and told him that he was afraid. He had never been afraid of anything in the woods before, yet for some reason he felt overtaken with fear. Both of them climbed down out of their stands and sat together on the ground for the remainder of the hunt.

At about 9:30 a.m., after seeing no sign of a deer, they decided to call it quits for the morning. Their plans were to go home, have lunch, and then return to the woods to hunt that afternoon. But like most young boys whose thoughts jump from one thing to another, Luke was thinking about duck hunting and a duck blind they had been working on that needed to be finished. (A duck blind is a camouflage obstruction used to hide behind while duck hunting.)

After returning home, Luke got permission from his dad, and he and a couple of his buddies left on the four-wheeler to go and work on the duck blind. He took his walkie-talkie with him so that he could be reached when lunch was ready.

Luke, along with his friends, Tyler and Colton, drove about a half mile across a field to a pond surrounded by a patch of woods where the blind was located.

They were well into the job when Colton got struck in the eye by a twig. Because his brother was in such pain, Tyler decided that he had better get him home so that their mom could check out the injury. Since the work on the duck blind was almost completed, Luke decided to stay behind and finish it, and then stop and check on Colton's injury on his way home.

Shortly after they had left, Luke received a call on the walkie-talkie. It was his father telling him that lunch would soon be ready and that he needed to start toward the house. He told his dad that he was almost finished and asked for permission to stop by and check on Colton on his way home. His dad said that it would be okay, but not to be long because the food would get cold. Luke promised, "I'll be there in about ten minutes."

Luke worked quickly to finish the project, and then got on his four-wheeler and started out of the woods. As Luke drove through the field on his way to his buddies' house, something malfunctioned on the four-wheeler that caused the front wheels to lock up. When that happened, Luke was thrown over the handlebars to the ground, onto his back. The four-wheeler then flipped end over end, and as it did, the carriage rack on the back of the vehicle struck Luke in the face.

Several minutes had passed, and Luke still hadn't shown up to check on Colton. The two boys felt that something must have happened. After trying to figure out what could have gone wrong, they quickly agreed that he might have had trouble with the four-wheeler not starting or something of that nature. It was out of character for him not to show up after telling them that he would do so.

They went in search of their friend and found him not far from where they had last seen him. To their horror, the first thing they saw was the wrecked four-wheeler, and their friend lying face down in a puddle of blood. Since Luke was lying face down, the boys didn't know the extent of the injury and that the carriage of the four-wheeler had struck him in the face.

Luke's friends could hear his father frantically calling for his son on the walkie-talkie, asking him where he was. Trembling, one of the boys got the walkie-talkie out of Luke's pocket and told his dad, "Luke is hurt bad, and he needs to get to the hospital."

By some miracle, when Jeff arrived, his son was still conscious. Jeff hurried to his son's side, noticing that Luke was choking on something. Jeff could only look on in shock as his son reached into his mouth and pulled out his top palate, complete with teeth. His whole top palate had been knocked loose, and it looked as if Luke were pulling a half set of dentures out of his mouth.

The four-wheeler had fallen with such force on Luke's face that the impact caused his skull to buckle and cave into his brain. The bones in his face were shattered. From his eyes downward, and from ear to ear, the skin had been torn from his face. The doctors told his family later that his tongue had come within an eighth of an inch from being severed. At that point the only thing keeping him alive was the mercy of God. His father later compared the damage to his son's face to a tomato that had been struck with a hammer.

Jeff picked up the broken body of his little eleven-year-old son and laid him in his pickup truck. He drove as fast as he could possibly drive to get his son to the hospital, all the while hoping and praying that his son would live.

Jeff had so many things going on in his mind while he was trying to get to the emergency room. He immediately called his wife and told her that she and the girls needed to pray because Luke had been in an accident and was hurt really bad. As he continued to drive, he couldn't help but think that just a few hours earlier these guys were sitting in the woods together waiting for that big buck to step out, and now his only son was fighting for his life.

On the way to the hospital Jeff drove at a very high rate of speed, flashing his lights, blowing his horn, and running up on the curbs. It was just the hand of God that kept them from crashing. All the while he was driving, he continually had to turn his son back and forth from his stomach to his back. He noticed that when Luke was on his back he would begin to choke on his blood, so Jeff would turn him on his stomach, allowing the blood to drain. Yet it was difficult for him to breathe on his stomach, so Jeff had to once again turn him on his back. This process continued until they finally reached the Claremore Regional Hospital.

The truck had become so overheated from the trip that it caught on fire while sitting under the awning at the emergency room. However, Jeff's only concern at the moment was getting his son help. Some of the guys standing nearby pushed the burning truck away from the building. The truck was severely damaged by the fire.

The staff at the emergency room was not prepared for what they were about to witness. Luke and his father were both soaked in blood as Jeff brought the little guy in, still wearing his hunting clothes from earlier that morning.

The attendants on duty were shocked, wondering how such a little body could withstand such a blow to the head and still be alive. Some who had worked in the emergency room for several years vowed that it was the worst case they had ever witnessed. There were those on the staff who actually passed out at the sight of the gruesome injury. Later, several of those working in the ER would require special counseling because of what they had experienced.

Due to the severity of the injury, the doctors at Claremore Regional Hospital quickly decided that Luke must be taken to the St. Francis Hospital in Tulsa, Oklahoma. Before he could be transported to Tulsa, a tracheotomy had to be performed to help him get air to breathe; then his almost lifeless body was loaded onto a helicopter, and he was on his way to Tulsa. It is about twenty-nine miles from the Claremore Regional Hospital to the St. Francis Hospital in Tulsa. Yet the drive seemed a lot farther. After the physicians at St. Francis Hospital examined Luke, they concluded that if he were to have any chance of survival, he must have brain surgery immediately. The excessive bleeding, however, prevented them from doing brain surgery. And since they couldn't get the bleeding to stop, their final words were, "We're just waiting on him to die."

The word of Luke's accident began to spread like wildfire throughout the church community; as a result, people began to flock to the hospital. At one point, the hospital security was called in because of the massive crowd that had gathered in the hall. The security people, not knowing the reason for the crowd, feared that some kind of a riot was about to break out.

The support from the local clergy was phenomenal. Approximately seventy-five ministers from all backgrounds and denominations knelt side-by-side in the prayer chapel and prayed for Luke and his family. Jeff Armbrister said that it was an awesome sight to see everyone pulling together on Luke's behalf.

Besides those ministers, there were about three hundred people in the waiting room and the surrounding area who came to show their love and support. A family that had so often reached out to others in need now had to draw strength and support from friends and family to help them through the most difficult time of their lives. One of the things that eased the horror of this terrible nightmare was the fact that so many people cared.

Later that evening, the bleeding miraculously stopped to the point that Luke could be taken into surgery. The surgeons removed a portion of his skull that had caved in; it left a hole about the size of a fist. Since the damage to the right lobe of Luke's brain was irreparable, it had to be removed.

After the surgery, the family was called together for some very devastating news. They were told that both of Luke's eardrums were severely damaged. Because of his injuries, his spinal fluid was draining out through his ears, and should they not be able to get that stopped, he would be facing paralysis. The horrible report continued as the doctors told the parents that the left side of their son's body would most likely become disabled since the right lobe of his brain had been removed. The family was informed that the right side of the brain not only controls the left side of the body, but it controls speech as well, which meant that their son would be unable to speak.

From everything they were hearing, a very bleak picture was being painted of Luke's future. Should he survive, the likelihood of him being brain damaged, deaf, blind, paralyzed, and not able to speak was almost certain. To put it bluntly, the doctors were concluding that he would basically be a vegetable, if he lived.

For several weeks before the accident, the Reverend Jeff Armbrister had been preaching and teaching faith in his evangelistic services. As a result of these messages, great things were happening in the lives of those who received the Word. Though he never realized it at the time, the messages and lessons he had been teaching and preaching on faith were especially meant for him and his family.

Jeff and his family were now "living examples" of James' teaching: "Knowing this, that the trying of your faith worketh patience" (James 1:3 KJV).

The Bible offers a long list of names of those whose faith had been severely tried and tested. A few that come to mind are Abraham, Joseph, Job, Daniel, Paul, and Peter. All these men were friends of God. They were all great men of faith, yet their faith was severely put to the test.

If this family could endure this test of faith that they were now going through, their names could very well be added to that long list of men of faith. They had given their entire lives to serving God, and now they were facing a giant, who would love nothing more than to destroy their faith. Up to this point, they had proven faithful and had not become angry or bitter. On the contrary, they continued to trust God for the full recovery of their son. However, the battle had just begun, and the outcome to this challenge was yet to be determined: Would this family be able to endure such a difficult test and continue their journey "through the fire" with unwavering faith?

Although the family was extremely tired, sleep was not an option. They were afraid that if they closed their eyes to sleep, Luke might be gone when they awakened. In fact, it was about eight days before Jeff could actually sleep. Every time he would close his eyes and try to rest he would see images of his precious son's battered face, and he would relive the horrible event all over again.

Luke remained in the hospital at Tulsa in a coma for fifteen days. Finally, the doctors got him stable enough to move him. He was then transported to the Children's Medical Hospital in Dallas, Texas. At this point, his family was still given very little hope for his survival. However, they remained by his side, continually praying and asking God for new miracles.

It was during that time that Jeff began to ask God over and over, "Why could it not have happened to me instead of my son?" The only answer he seemed to get was that he could not have handled it.

The physicians had warned the family what to expect should Luke come out of the coma. They were told that about 95 percent of the people waking from a methadone coma react very violently: screaming, cursing, and often fighting. Ever since the accident Karen's prayer was that when her son came out from under the coma and medication he would be the same young man that he was before the accident. Her prayers were answered; the first words out of his mouth were, "I love you Mom, with all of my heart."

The Armbrister family will always remember February 8, 2001, as a day of miracles. This was the day that Luke was released from the Children's Medical Hospital in Dallas. Some thought that this day would never come, but Luke's family, along with many others, had never given up hope. Contrary to what the doctors had predicted, on the day their son left the hospital, not only could he walk, but also he could talk, he could see, and he could hear. Because of the grace of God, this family was ready to move on with their lives. They were now more determined than ever to turn this test into a testimony.

What an awesome thing it was to be back in Claremore, Oklahoma. After what this family had gone through for the last three months, it was a huge understatement to say, "There is no place like home." It was a wonderful day.

For almost three months everyone in the family, including Jeff, Karen, Samantha, and Celeste, had spent all their time at the hospital. After such a long period, with no work and very little money coming in, their funds were basically depleted.

Karen was told about a church that was assisting people with food. Several people encouraged her to go there for some assistance. At first she was hesitant to go. This family had always been givers, helping others. They had never before been in this kind of a situation, where they had to be on the receiving end.

Karen felt broken as she and Luke drove to the church. There were so many questions going through her mind: "Haven't we been through enough? Haven't I proven my humility? What's next? Do I really have to go through this food line?"

Unaware that those receiving aid were supposed to park in the back of the church, Karen parked the car in the front, and helped Luke out of the car because he was still unable to get out of the car on his own. As they made their way to the church, a kind gentleman, who introduced himself as the assistant pastor, greeted them. The minister reached out his hand and said, "You must be Luke Armbrister."

Luke, barely able to speak, said, "Yes sir, I am."

They talked for a while, and though Luke was still so weak and very broken from the accident, he tried to laugh and act in a courteous manner toward the gentleman who was doing his best to assist them. The minister directed them to the food line, and then he left.

After receiving the food items, Karen shed quite a few tears on the way home. Though she was very grateful, at the same time, she had learned a new lesson in humility. Her family had never had to take handouts before. She recognized, however, that this was just another step in their long journey "through the fire," and she had the feeling that they still had a long way to go.

About two months later, they attended an auction in town, just as something to do to get themselves and Luke out of the house. While at the auction, a lady approached Karen and said, "Mrs. Armbrister, I feel that I must share something with you."

"Sure," Karen replied.

"Do you remember going to a particular church and talking to a man who was the assistant pastor?" the lady continued.

"Yes," Karen said, "I sure do. I remember it very well."

The lady commenced to share her story:

> You never know how God is going to work. The man that greeted you and let you in the church is our assistant pastor, and he serves as our young adult Sunday school teacher as well. The following Sunday after you and Luke had been there, he came into the classroom crying and very emotional. He said, 'For our lesson today, I'm going to talk about Luke Armbrister. One morning last week I told God, I'm through; I'm giving it up; I can't take it anymore; I am quitting.'
>
> He continued to tell his class that Luke Armbrister and his mother showed up at the front door of the church. He said that after he had talked with that young man, he felt something that he had not felt in such a long time, and that he was overtaken with conviction. After helping them to the food line, he said, he fell on his face in prayer, weeping before God and saying, "If that young man can make it, so can I." He said that he wept and prayed for over an hour and a half.

After hearing this story, Karen told God that she was sorry for complaining. She could clearly see that God had sent them there on behalf of that minister who was ready to throw his hands up and quit. God had taken Luke's test and turned it into a testimony, which helped that man find the strength that he needed to be strong and to continue in his work for the Lord.

Several months after getting out of the hospital, some of Luke's friends invited him to go to a Crabb Family concert. What a treat is was for him to get out and do some of the things that he had enjoyed doing before the accident.

Luke had been to a Crabb Family concert just a few months before the accident and had really enjoyed the group; he especially enjoyed Jason's singing.

After about an hour into the concert, we began to sing "Through the Fire." When Luke heard the line, "Help will always come in time," the strangest feeling came over him. As he began to share with his mother why he felt as he did about those lyrics, all she could do was weep. Luke proceeded to tell her that before the accident he had heard "Through the Fire" only one time. It was when he and his family had driven to Muskogee.

Although he had only heard the song one time, while he was unconscious in a comatose state, he could hear those words over and over: "Help will always come in time. Help will always come in time." Those words seemed to cheer him on. They were the very words of encouragement he needed, reassuring him that help was on the way.

Luke shared another experience that he had while in the hospital. During the time that he was unconscious, he could remember having horrible, recurring nightmares. As he put it, "I was terrified. I wanted to call out for Mom and Dad, but I couldn't. All I could do was pray in my mind, saying, 'Jesus, will you come and sit by me?'" He said, "I remember the feeling that someone had laid down beside me, and I could feel his nail-scarred hand as it took hold of mine." Luke said that after that experience, he never had another nightmare.

Luke has had many hurdles to overcome since the accident. He dealt with withdrawals from the morphine and methadone for several months.

While sitting, at times his legs would begin to jump and twitch. His dad would massage the muscles in the back of his legs to help calm them down.

In a period of nine years he has had seventy-two reconstructive surgeries; his first surgery lasted seventeen hours. With the reconstructing of Luke's mouth, jaws, gums, nose, lips, palate and the scar tissue on his tongue, normal eating has been impossible. Therefore, a feeding tube has fed him in his stomach. Luke's parents had been told that their son would never be able to drink liquids. Miraculously, however, he has been able to drink liquids since 2002.

It has been a difficult journey, but new miracles seem to appear around every corner.

Through it all, Luke states that he can't ever remember getting mad at God or blaming Him. He never once asked God why He had allowed him to be put through such a trial. It has been often said, "Trials usually do one of two things; they make you bitter or better." There is definitely no bitterness toward God from Luke.

One time I asked Luke, "What has this experience done to your faith?"

His reply was, "I have found out, there is nothing that God cannot do, and there is nothing that God will not do for you." He said, "All my life my father has taught faith, and as a result, we have seen some wonderful things happen in the lives of other people. But now, I know from first-hand experience that God can and that God will."

There have been times when any chance of Luke living a normal life looked hopeless. At one point the question was not, "Would Luke ever hunt again?" The main concern was, "Will he ever walk again?"

He did both. Five years after the accident, Luke killed his first deer; it was a ten-point buck. His father was there to share the joy with him. That big buck's head is mounted and is hanging on his wall—just one more victory in this long journey "through the fire."

Jeff is now the pastor of a homeless outreach mission. Volunteers bus homeless people from inner city Tulsa to the mission. Each Sunday they transport between thirty and one hundred homeless people to the mission. Some of those ministered to are drug addicts, gang members, prostitutes, or even murderers, but none are turned away.

At the mission, participants first attend a church service where they hear the Word of God and are instructed on how to receive Jesus Christ as their Lord and Savior. Then they receive a hot meal and visit the clothing bank where they can pick out some nice clothes. Luke said that on many occasions he has seen those who had attended the mission the previous Sunday proudly wearing their new clothes the following Sunday.

Within a period of about two and a half years the ministry has seen more than fifteen hundred people accept Jesus as their Lord and Savior. Of that number, approximately three hundred are now off the streets, working and living normal lives. Many have gone back home to live with their families.

The mission did a Christmas program for the homeless one week before Christmas 2009. A special program was presented in which there was a guest choir. The homeless were fed a good meal, and each one received a gift package containing a new coat, a new blanket, socks, gloves, underclothes, and many other essential items. There were 430 homeless in attendance; it was a great day.

The day that Luke was released from the hospital in Dallas, he felt that God had called him to be a minister of the gospel. Since then it has become his passion to share the gospel message and the goodness of God with anyone who will listen. One Sunday Pastor Jeff had asked his son to minister at the mission. He was very eager to do so. A certain lady in the congregation had been coming to the mission for about two months, mostly for the food and clothing. On the morning that Luke ministered, conviction gripped her heart, and she came forward and accepted Christ as her Savior. Since then she has been miraculously reunited with her husband and children. She and her family now faithfully attend the regular church services.

From time to time the mission will feature guest speakers. In one particular service, Pastor Jeff asked his congregation who their favorite guest speakers were. When I asked Luke about the response to his dad's question, he replied: "Not to brag on myself, but of all the many speakers that had been there, I was in the top three."

What an example this young man is, now twenty-two years old as of this writing. What a testimony for the kingdom of God. He is not looking for sympathy, or pity. He is merely looking for someone who will listen as he shares with them what the Lord has done for him and his family.

The world is always searching for a hero—someone to look up to that will be a good role model for his or her children. This is your guy: Luke Armbrister.

One time I asked Luke, "Having come through all that you have, what advice would you give to a person facing a 'through the fire' experience in his or her life?"

His reply was, "Pray, believe, trust God, and hold on 'cause 'help will always come in time.'"

Conclusion

Our Lord Will Show Up

It appears that some people's greatest ministry is their testimony. They become a display and living proof of deliverance and the precious grace of God.

I can recall a lady in eastern Kentucky who would often sing a song that said, "The testing time will come."

Trying times come to everyone no matter what his or her status in life—sickness, financial crises, disappointment, and even death. I have never met anyone who hasn't walked the dreary road of frustration. We find that to be so true when we look at the story of Bob Bain, that brave soldier of the cross.

The greatest desire in his life was to work in the Kingdom of God, yet he struggled severely to do so. God doesn't always spare you the trial or take you around it; sometimes He walks you right through it.

If we knew in advance about the fiery trials that lie ahead of us we would be unable to sleep tonight; we would possibly have a nervous breakdown, or lose our mind. We couldn't handle it. Instead God gives us grace for the moment. How often has it been said: "If it had not been for the Lord who was on my side, I could never have made it."

If the McGuffey family had known in advance what was on the horizon, they possibly couldn't have handled it, yet God knew in His infinite wisdom; therefore He had grace waiting to help them cross the bridge of despair when their daughter, Autumn, died.

We must keep in mind that no matter how unbearable the furnace might seem to be, God's hand is on the thermostat. He will not allow more to be put on us than we can bear.

Trials are spawned from many different situations. Three things come to mind: Trials that are self-inflicted, trials beyond our control, and trials that are allowed by God.

If we would be honest with ourselves, we would have to agree that many trials are self-inflicted. We blame other people and situations when the fact is that we made a bad choice, took the wrong path, or even gave in to temptation. The consequences often set the stage for a painful "self-inflicted trial."

What better example is there than King David, who yielded to temptation and committed adultery with another man's wife. It spiraled out of control; the outcome was the ending of two lives, that of Uriah, Bathsheba's husband, and the son who was born as a result of the adulterous affair. It caused David much grief and shame.

Other trials come as a result of things beyond our control; they are brought about by circumstances such as disasters, sickness, a bad economy, and even the choices made by others that can throw you into a trying time in your life.

This type of trial was faced by a young lady about eleven years old, whom I met when I preached at a church in Hot Springs, Arkansas, one Sunday morning. Prior to the service, the church's pastor had informed me that I was going to receive a very special surprise. I anxiously waited, and just before I was called to the platform the young lady was introduced to the congregation.

You could sense that something very special was about to take place; there was an awesome presence of God that seemed to settle over the congregation. Immediately following the girl's introduction, the sound technician began playing a music track that I was very familiar with.

The song was "Through the Fire." I was expecting the girl to sing along with the soundtrack just as I had witnessed others do many times before. Instead she began doing sign language to a recorded version of the song. I felt very honored; her sincerity was very evident and much practice had gone into the routine.

A minister sitting behind me leaned forward and told me a heart-wrenching story. He briefed me on what had taken place less than a year earlier. The girl and her mother had discovered her deceased father. It was apparent that he had committed suicide. I was later informed that he had battled a drug addiction for many years. There are no words to explain what I felt as I watched and listened in tears.

I publicly thanked her for what she had done and how that it was one of the greatest honors that I had ever received.

At the conclusion of my message I gave an invitation to those who would like to come forward for prayer; immediately she responded and came forward. I prayed with her and then sat down with her as I embraced her; both of us wept. I said to her, "I wrote the lyrics to that song, 'Through the Fire,' many years ago, but I have found out today for whom it was written." I said to her, "This is your song. It was written for you. Take these words and use them whenever you need them."

The dark trial that she was passing through was no fault of her own. Yet it was evident that God was walking her through it, each step of the way.

Then there are those trials that God allows; the first person that comes to mind is Job.

I have often said that if we think we are having a bad day that can't get any worse, we just need to read the first chapter of the Book of Job in the Bible. It just seems to make you feel better. What a trial that man and his wife encountered. It wasn't self-inflicted, and it wasn't caused by circumstances around them. It was allowed by Almighty God.

God could have disallowed it, yet He trusted Job enough to allow him to be put to the test.

It is very clear that Satan had to ask God to lower the hedge, because Job was under divine protection, and Satan couldn't even touch or get to him without divine permission.

Looking back over the tribulation of Job, we know that in the end he was blessed and restored greater than ever. Yet throughout the ordeal he found himself confused and frustrated many times. He didn't understand what was going on. After all, the Bible says he was a perfect man, a praying man, and a man that resisted evil and feared God.

Job couldn't see the battle raging against him; it was in the spirit world. He couldn't figure out what was going on. The scripture says, however, that through it all, Job never sinned or charged God foolishly.

Wow! What a powerful testimony. Doesn't that make you want to find out how he did it?

Through his fiery trial Job made statements like everyone else does in similar situations; for instance,

- More than once, he wished he'd never been born.
- He wished that God would grant him one request and Take his life.
- He earnestly prayed for deliverance.
- He could not understand what was going on.
- At times he thought that God was punishing him.
- At times he thought that God was angry with him.

He went from being rich, powerful, fruitful, blessed, highly favored, and the father of seven sons and three daughters, to being homeless, broke, childless, disabled and friendless within a few hours.

Yet he worshiped and declared, "Naked came I out of my mother's womb, and naked shall I return thither: the LORD gave, and the LORD hath taken away; blessed be the name of the LORD." Wow, what a statement of faith.

Right in the middle of his grueling, almost unbearable situation, his wife made a stunning statement: "Why don't you curse God and die." Now, how would you deal with that, combined with everything else? Because of the remark made to her suffering husband, we have made some cruel statements and remarks concerning that "ruthless" woman, Job's wife. Yet, have we been too quick to jump the gun? Have we ever considered Job's wife?

This was her tribulation, too. Maybe she was nearing a mental breakdown. These were real people just like you and me. Could it be that she had reached the point that she couldn't stand to see him suffer any longer? Maybe her nerves were so frazzled that her judgment wasn't quite up to par.

Think about it—everything he lost was her loss too. The ten children whom they had just buried were her babies, whom she had given birth to. Her livelihood had been taken; it was her home that lay in ashes; it was her husband that was unable to rise and rebuild. She had to have been under tremendous pressure. Could it be that she thought it was the only thing left to end the suffering? We do know that her loyalty was such that she didn't just walk off and abandon Job.

This was one of the darkest trials that we will ever read about. It all happened so fast, so unexpectedly, without warning, and defiantly without understanding. Their frustration level must have been at peak level.

Yet, they made it through.

They made it without a Bible to help them understand what was going on, no TV evangelist offering a book or a set of audio teaching series on how to make it through, no survival kit, no psychologists, no therapists, no psychiatrists. They had no help from friends, and no support from the Church, yet they made it. Minute by minute, hour by hour, day by day, they made it.

The key thing that kept Job strong was "*trust.*" Job stated, "Yet will I trust him."

Trust is a different element than faith, though very similar.

According to the Bible we are dealt a measure of faith from God. Faith also comes by hearing or reading the word of God—we hear and we believe.

On the other hand, trust is earned in someone; it comes by experience. You can't trust something that hasn't been proved.

I remember that when my children were small I would stand them on the table and tell them to jump and I would catch them. They were somewhat hesitant at first, but after they had jumped a couple of times and I had caught them, I had earned their trust. It wasn't long until they would jump with their eyes closed; they knew that Dad would catch them.

Somewhere in Job's life he had learned to trust God. He had jumped and God had caught him.

Life is filled with so many questions: Why parents have to be taken in death? Why some children must die in the prime of their lives.

Recently, tornadoes ripped through many parts of the United States. Hundreds of lives were lost—young and old, saints and sinners. The rich and poor were left devastated. Churches, businesses, schools, and homes were destroyed. There were many questions; the greatest of all was: Why?

Yet Jesus said, "It rains on the just and on the unjust."

No one is exempt. Even though we can't understand why, it is a fact that bad things happen to good people. We will never have the answer to every question in life, but we must trust the omniscient God.

No matter what kind of trial you may be going through, the words of the song continue to ring true:

> He never promised that the cross would not get heavy,
> And the hill would not be hard to climb.
> He never offered our victories without fighting,
> But he said help would always come in time.
> Just remember when you're standing in the valley of decision,
> And the adversary says give in.
> Just hold on, our Lord will show up,
> And he will take you through the fire again.

You can count on it! Our God is faithful!

Acknowledgments

Writing this book has been a totally different experience from writing songs.

I entered into this new adventure about five years ago, in 2006.

I soon discovered that I needed some help; everyone I asked was truly gracious with their participation and assistance.

A special thanks goes to my wife Debi. She labored for many hours typing for me, as I would read to her my notes. Thanks for her patience as I would get into my "zone" and be oblivious for days to everything going on around me. Debi, I love you.

Thanks to my dear friend Ralph Doiron, you were a miracle worker; you gave structure to my manuscript and made it readable.

Thanks to all the families who supplied the information for these stories; you were so willing to share your heart and soul.

Thanks specifically to Dianne, Cathy, Eddie, Jeff, Karen, Luke, Stephanie, John, Marcia, Cas, Levi, Rebecca, Joey, and Jim—all of you were awesome to work with.

Thanks to my Lord and Savior, who put it in my spirit to share these powerful stories and who gave me the determination to see this project through.

About the Author

Gerald Crabb was born in Rosine, Kentucky, a rural town, which is also the birthplace of Bill Monroe, the founder of bluegrass music.

Gerald began his ministry and preached his first sermon in a small church near Horse Branch, Kentucky, in the summer of 1973 at age sixteen. Since then he has pastored seven churches—two of which he founded.

He has written more than four hundred songs and has had twenty-two national-charted number one songs.

In 1994, he founded the internationally known group, The Crabb Family.

Gerald has won multiple awards for his songwriting, including the following:

- 2002 BMI Songwriter of the Year
- 2004 and 2005 SGMG (Southern Gospel Music Guild) Awards Songwriter of the Year
- 2005 and 2008 SGN (Southern Gospel News) Awards Songwriter of the Year
- 2005, 2007, and 2010 Diamond Awards Songwriter of the Year
- 42nd Annual 2011 Dove Awards Songwriter of the Year

In 2002 Gerald was honored by BMI as publisher of the year in Christian music. Also, Gerald has received six Performance awards from BMI.

Gerald's songs have generated many other awards, including the following:

- ⚔ 2003 Dove Award: Southern Gospel Song of the Year, for "Don't You Wanna Go"
- ⚔ 2004 Dove Award: Southern Gospel Song of the Year, for "The Cross"
- ⚔ 2005 Dove Award: Southern Gospel Song of the Year, for "He Came Looking For Me"
- ⚔ 2005 Dove Award: Country Recorded Song of the Year, for "Forever"
- ⚔ 2005 Dove Award: Traditional Gospel Recorded Song of the Year, for "Through the Fire"
- ⚔ 2005 SGN Music Award: Song of the Year, for "He Came Looking For Me"
- ⚔ 2005 SGN Music Award: Progressive Song of the Year, for "Greater Is He"
- ⚔ 2006 Dove Award: Southern Gospel Song of the Year, for "Through the Fire"
- ⚔ 2007 SGM (Southern Gospel Music) Fan Award, for "Hold Me While I Cry"
- ⚔ 2011 Diamond Award: Song of the Year, for "Please Forgive Me"
- ⚔ 2011 Dove Award: Song of The Year, for "Sometimes I Cry"

Songs written by Gerald have been recorded by such artists as The Crabb Family, Randy Travis, Marie Osmond, Jason Crabb, Larry Sparks, The Gaither Vocal Band, The Brooklyn Tabernacle Choir, Donny McClurkin, Michael English, Rev. Richard Roberts, Ivan Parker, The Talley Trio, The Hoppers, Marty Raybon, Karen Peck, and many others.

Many of Gerald's songs have been featured on the *Gaither Homecoming* videos.

Gerald's songs have been performed on international networks including NBC (on *The Today Show*), Fox News Network, Trinity Broadcasting Network (TBN), The Christian Broadcasting Network (on *The 700 Club*), The Inspiration Network (INSP), Daystar Christian Network, Country Music Television (CMT), Great American Country (GAC), and The Gospel Music Channel.

Gerald's songs have been performed at such places as Carnegie Hall, The Grand Ole Opry House, The Ryman Auditorium, and Red Rocks Amphitheatre, as well as churches and concert venues around the United States.

Gerald and his wife, Debi, make their home in Ripley, Mississippi. They schedule and conduct approximately one hundred and fifty dates per year, which include concerts, camp meetings, and revivals.

Website: www.geraldcrabb.net